Return of the Court

JESTERS

Back to the Bar for More of the Funniest Stories from Canada's Courts

PETER V. MacDONALD, Q.C.

FOREWORD BY
WILLARD Z. ESTEY, Q.C.

Stoddart

For
my contributors
(God bless 'em!)

First published in 1990 by
Stoddart Publishing Co. Limited
34 Lesmill Road
Toronto, Canada
M3B 2T6

Canadian Cataloguing in Publication Data

MacDonald, Peter V. (Peter Vincent), 1934–
    Return of the court jesters

ISBN 0-7737-2438-9

1. Law – Canada – Anecdotes.   2. Courts – Canada –
Anecdotes.   I. Title.

K184.7.C3M333 1990   349.71'0207   C90-094763-2

Some of the American anecdotes appearing in chapters 2, 9,
10, and 11 are copyrighted by the National Shorthand
Reporters Association of Vienna, Virginia, and are reprinted
with its permission.

Printed and bound in the United States of America

CONTENTS

FOREWORD

One day, the great Aimé Geoffrion was addressing the Supreme Court of Canada, presided over by the Chief Justice, Sir Lyman Duff. Mr. Geoffrion was most anxious to put before the Court, and to force them to direct their minds to, the precise wording of a rather lengthy federal statute. Sir Lyman interrupted repeatedly, stating that they had all read the statute and were familiar with it, although he did admit that he had not examined the entire lengthy section in question, including all the subsections. Mr. Geoffrion cheerfully replied, "Very well, then, let us all read it together." He thereupon proceeded to read to the Court the entire section which represented, as it turned out, 90 percent of what he had to say on appeal. By a little wit and persistence he quickly had their full attention.

Humor, by itself, is humorless. The point of a presentation by counsel is to achieve success by persuasive techniques. Usually, such humor as creeps into the hearing process is a product of a spur-of-the moment response. Artificially inserted humor serves no purpose as very few in the courtroom have come to be entertained. On the other hand, it is a fact of our community life that a great volume of human comedy is produced spontaneously on the judicial stage. It is, by itself, entertaining to the Bar and the general public. It is not humorous material to be employed in subsequent court proceedings. It is in the latter sense that this book makes its contribution. It is a collection of courtroom lore, from Canada and around the English-speaking world, which provides an insight into both the judicial process and the role of the Courts in the community. At the same time, it is a source of entertainment right across the community.

The author has, with great effort, collected for succeeding generations some of the interesting and comical moments in our judicial history. His stories are illustrations of the vagaries of human conduct under the stress and strain of the courtroom. In their own way they deliver the message that nothing can usefully be introduced into the trial or judicial hearing which interferes with the flow of fact and law upon which that process depends, nor which deflects the tribunal from its appointed task, unless it is a flash of wit. In short, it must not be forgotten that justice, not comedy, is a product of the courtroom. Nevertheless, the spark of humor often represents the turning point in the eternal contests between counsel and witness, and in a different sense, between counsel and the court.

This book serves well the two purposes: entertainment coming naturally from roots in our community and subtle instruction here and there on the proper place and use for wit in the judicial process.

WILLARD Z. ESTEY

PREFACE

Before unleashing a brand-new and unruly mob of court jesters on a laugh-crazed public, I wish to turn the spotlight on the many hundreds of generous folks who made these periodic jamborees possible. I refer, of course, to my vast network of contributors, to whom this book is gratefully dedicated. They're all busy people, these benefactors, and they stretch from coast to coast — and occasionally beyond. They're listed at the back of this volume, and I ask that all of them stand up, right now, and take a long, swooping bow.

Since 1984, when I started collecting true, humorous courtroom anecdotes, I've skewered and preserved thousands of funny legal yarns — more, I'm sure, than anyone else on this planet — and, thanks to the readers of my books and newspaper columns, they're still coming in at a pretty steady clip. About 80 percent of my stories are mailed to me, and it's obvious from the thousands of letters I've received that a hell of a lot of people want laughter at regular intervals. Well, they've come to the right place.

Many of my correspondents have reported that my stories rid them of depression. Indeed, a memorable missive from a man in British Columbia stated: "Your book worked wondrous therapy on my monomanias, cured my disphoria and healed my psychic wounds. You should be arraigned for practicing psychiatry without a licence." Now that's the kind of rap I'll gladly plead guilty to, any time they lay it on me.

Other readers informed me that the anecdotes I presented triggered uncontrollable giggling, which caused their recent surgical stitches to pop. I also received numerous reports of marital discord caused by spouses — of both genders — reading aloud and laughing like hyenas at 3 A.M. and refusing to douse the light.

Various others tried to blame me for their aches and pains, like the New Brunswick lawyer who wrote: "I was laughing so much that I was crying most of the time. At one-thirty this morning I was so tired, and hurting so much in the ribs, that I had to go to bed and rest. I must have spent over three thousand calories reading Part One alone!" Now who would have thought that my books could lead to weight loss?

And, I ask you, how was I supposed to know that my literary efforts could sabotage a fellow's internal plumbing? The man in question wrote to me as follows: "My brother and his wife gave me *Court Jesters* for Christmas. 'Hah,' I said to myself, 'a good book for the john!' Except that, when trying to do my duty, I'd laugh so hard that the purpose of the trip would be forgotten and the urge would disappear. A few days of this and I decided that if I didn't want a king-size case of constipation I'd better relegate the book to the living room, where it is now."

As if sending funny stories weren't enough, most of my correspondents started or ended their letters with words of appreciation and encouragement. There's a prodigious amount of work involved in producing these books — countless lonely hours of digging, persuading, collecting, selecting, writing, rewriting — and with so many other things to do, it would have been easy to chuck the whole thing. But those encouraging letters kept spurring me on — letters written, for the most part, by wonderful strangers whom I'll never meet. While thanking me for restoring their perspective, they were, ironically, restoring *mine*!

Naturally, most of the letters I receive come from lawyers and judges and others involved in the legal world. But a great many people who have nothing to do with that world also write to me, and they keep telling me that my stories have shown them "the human side" of judges and lawyers. "The administration of justice is certainly one that comes under a lot of criticism," wrote a Fredericton woman, "but your efforts have given many of us food for thought — you are, after all, human beings!"

As a lawyer, and the son of a judge, I am greatly pleased by such an endorsement. How many people can say that they're human beings? Why, if this sort of recognition persists it will surely turn our heads — and then we'll probably be branded as inhuman all over again.

No one could ever speak that way about the wise and witty gentleman who kindly consented to write the Foreword to this book, the Honorable Willard Z. ("Buz") Estey, former Chief Justice of Ontario and recently retired Justice of the Supreme Court of Canada. "His Budship," as I've dubbed him, is a legal superstar and a warm and humorous man. I'm deeply honored to have him aboard.

With the exception of yours truly, no one was closer to this book, or contributed more to it, than my dear wife Catherine. As was the case with my two earlier volumes, Catherine was in on things from the beginning: reading hundreds of letters that contained funny stories, helping to select the ones that most merited publication, serving as a patient and indispensable sounding-board for my ideas, dispensing wise advice, and, most important of all, spurring me on with her loving and unceasing encouragement.

My children, Michael, Shaun, and Mary, rendered valuable assistance, too, by permitting the author-in-residence to regale them with newly arrived anecdotes and thereby assess the likely response of other young adults if said stories were later passed on to the public. Mary also helped her unmechanical Dad conquer his dread of the family word processor, to the point where he can now make it do what he wants it to do, most of the time.

I appreciate the assistance I received from a trio of secretaries: Karen Glasser, Charlotte Valles, and Sheila Stephenson. My thanks also to a quartet of court reporters who supplied me with court transcripts and urged colleagues to do likewise: Doreen Johnson, Gail McGilvray, Maria Mihailovich, and Ellen Vezina.

A a hearty thank-you to a former court reporter, Mary Louise Gilman, of Hanover, Massachusetts, for the assistance and encouragement she has given me over the past five years. Mrs. Gilman is a former editor of *The National Shorthand Reporter* and the editor of two books of humorous courtroom remarks, *Humor in the Court* and *More Humor in the Court*.

For services above and beyond the call of duty, special kudos go to Judge C.C. Barnett, Boris Krivy, Q.C., Colin D. McKinnon, Q.C., David N. Muise, John L. Hughes, and Ronald A. ("Ernie") Banks. I'm grateful for the assistance provided by law librarians Theresa Roth, Karen Teasdale, Sheila Hathorn, Jeff Shulman, and Diana Simpson.

A tip of the hat, too, to Angel Guerra, Bill Hanna, Donald G. Bastian, and Cy Strom, four helpful fellows at Stoddart Publishing.

And now, by popular demand, the return of the court jesters!

PETER V. MACDONALD
Hanover, Ontario

1

Hi Ho, Hi Ho,
It's Off To Court We Go!

THE MIRTH AND FUN GREW FAST AND FURIOUS.

Robert Burns

ONE MEMORABLE MORNING, a few years back, a visiting San Diego attorney dropped into a crowded Winnipeg criminal court to see how things were done north of the forty-ninth parallel. He'd picked the right day to come a-calling.

Festivities had not yet begun and the courtroom hummed with the usual sounds of lawyers, clients, witnesses, and spectators chatting and moving about.

When the judge appeared, promptly at ten, the court clerk shuffled to his feet and shouted the time-honored proclamation:

"Order, please!"

A split second later, a man awaiting trial bellowed back:

"A cheeseburger and fries!"

In a Newfoundland courtroom, at the start of a fresh new day, a man charged with swiping an oil-delivery truck was anxiously scanning the crowd, looking for his lawyer. He was mighty concerned because court was about to start and his counsel still hadn't made the scene.

A few moments later, in the nick of time, the lawyer came chugging into court, his eyes darting hither and yon as he tried to locate his client. Then he realized he couldn't remember what his client looked like, so he called out the fellow's name:

"Maxwell House!"

Like lightning, some wit at the back of the room yelled: "Caffeinated or decaffeinated?"

Such mirthful interjections, though not epidemic, are perpetrated from time to time in our ever-so-solemn courts. And, fortunately, so are other forms of merriment.

Yes, indeed, levity is no stranger to the courtroom, which has been called — and rightly so — "the best free show in town." Why, if laughter never raised its lovely head, many folks involved in the deadly serious business of dispensing justice might very well flip their wigs. A giggle or a guffaw can ease tensions, relieve boredom, restore perspective, and revive sagging spirits. As stated in the Book of Proverbs: "A merry heart doeth good like a medicine."

So let's dive into the medicine chest, shall we?

You just never know what will crop up in a court of law. Mr. Justice Paul Godin, of the Court of Queen's Bench of New Brunswick, treats us to a dandy yarn.

"I hate sentencing," His Lordship told me recently. "I have to gear myself up — psych myself up — to do it.

"In a case I tried not long ago, I convicted a man of a serious offense. I thought long and hard about sentencing and decided that the accused deserved no less than three years. I *had* to do it. I had resolved to do it, and I went into court *to* do it.

"The accused was in the prisoner's dock, and in the audience I saw his wife, who was actually nursing a baby! I had never seen that sort of thing in court.

"That really got to me. I couldn't proceed with three years. I cut it back to eighteen months.

"I went back to my office, took off my gown, and tried to forget about what I'd done. A few moments later, the sheriff, who'd been in court, came into my office and said, 'Oh, by the way, My Lord, that wasn't his wife and that wasn't her baby!'"

David L. Youngson, a veteran Vancouver lawyer, takes us back to the 1950s for a memorable moment — to wit, the inauspicious start he got in law.

"At the outset of my legal career," Youngson writes, "I defended a client who was charged with being a 'peeping Tom.'

"As identification was at issue, my client sat in the public gallery. The complainant, when called upon to identify the accused, did not hesitate in pointing to *me*. I then decided to engage in civil practice."

In 1966, a good friend of mine, federal prosecutor Orval J. Troy, Q.C., made what has to be the funniest entrance ever made by a lawyer in any courtroom anywhere.

On the eve of his first appearance in court in the Northwest Territories, at a chilly spot called Hay River, Orval did what he always did before hitting the sack. He put his dentures in a glass of water and turned out the light.

The temperature plummeted during the night and when he awoke he was shocked to see that his choppers were encased in a solid block of ice. Not only that, but he had to scamper to make court in time.

A few minutes later the courtroom erupted in laughter as Orval stood, glass in hand, trying to request an emergency recess so he could thaw out his teeth. The problem was that he couldn't make himself understood.

Finally, after pointing a few times to his mouth and the glass, his charade paid off and the judge adjourned court so that the new Crown Attorney could attend to his dentures. In the washroom, a steady stream of hot water did the trick and the *real* Orval Troy then got down to business.

After many years of outstanding work in the far north, the fellow with the frozen teeth went on to become a judge of the Territorial Court of the Northwest Territories, responsible for bringing justice to the entire eastern Arctic. I'm advised, and verily believe, that he's had no further trouble with his choppers.

Truth is stranger than fiction, they say. Sometimes it's a lot funnier, too. Just ask Dahn Batchelor.

He knows. Boy, does he know!

Dahn, a Toronto criminologist, was the "star" of a slapstick caper that's straight out of "Night Court." And, good sport that he is, he wrote to tell us all about it:

"In May of 1988, Toronto lawyer Robert Hopkins and I attended a trial in Belleville in which he was acting for a man who was charged with impaired driving. Bob asked me to investigate the circumstances of his client's arrest and had planned to call me as an expert witness.

"When we arrived at court we discovered that it was packed with high-school students who were there to learn how criminal trials are conducted.

"My experience in court as an expert witness has shown me that if a witness is well dressed the trial judge is more apt to listen to what he has to say. So I dressed in a dark three-piece suit (as always) and sat up at the counsel table for all to admire.

"During a lengthy discussion between the judge and the lawyers, I decided to go to the washroom. When I returned, I heard some laughing from the spectators. I figured that I had missed a joke and waited with anticipation for the next one.

"About a minute after I sat down, the accused walked over to the counsel table and whispered in my ear: 'Dahn, don't look now but your white suspenders are hanging down around your knees.'

"What does an expert witness who is trying to impress everyone in the courtroom do when he learns that nearly every eye in that courtroom is on him? I tried what Houdini would never have attempted. I tried to slip my suspenders over my shoulders without taking off my jacket and vest.

"The judge was transfixed at watching me attempt the impossible. The Crown Attorney later said that it was the highlight of the trial.

"Bob was still oblivious to what was going on beside him, other than the fact that I kept jabbing him with my elbow as I tried my impossible maneuvers. His whispered words — 'Keep still!' — could be heard by everyone. The more he whispered, the more they laughed.

"After concluding that I had to partially disrobe, I did so — and then began slipping the left suspender over my shoulder. Bob could take no more. He turned abruptly and faced me with a scowl. Then his expression turned to one of utter surprise.

"There I was, my left arm out of my jacket and vest, with the suspender in the air, just ready to snap onto my shoulder.

"Bob turned to the judge, then looked me right in the eye and said in a voice that could be heard in every corner of the courtroom: 'You can take him anywhere, but you can't dress him!'

"We won the case, but I will never know if the judge took me seriously when I gave my evidence. He kept smiling all through my testimony."

Some of the fact-situations that courts have to deal with are ludicrous, to put it mildly. On June 11, 1975, Vancouver lawyer Joel A. Kerbel defended a man who was charged with "committing an indecent act in a public place." It was a case he'll never forget.

"A department store detective testified that he observed two washroom cubicles, with a man in each cubicle, and noticed one man crouched down, facing the partition wall, extending his penis under the partition, in the sixteen-inch space between the floor and the bottom of the partition," says Kerbel, who now practices in Toronto. "He claimed he observed this activity through 'a slit in the door.'

"The evidence was that the partition was about two inches thick, the accused's body was about eight or ten inches away from the partition, and three or four inches of his penis protruded into the adjoining cubicle.

"I submitted that the offense was most unlikely because in order to find the accused guilty, the judge would have to make a rather 'long assumption.' If the detective's evidence was believed, the accused's penis was at least fourteen inches long."

You'd think such a well-reasoned argument would create plenty of reasonable doubt and result in a victory for the accused. But Judge D. D. Hume — in effect, stretching a point — ruled as follows:

"I find the accused guilty as charged. I appreciate the apparent difficulty which some of the evidence suggests there might have been for the accused to commit this act. It does seem, mathematically, that if his thighs are seventeen inches from knee to groin and he was upright against the partition, that to effect his penis underneath the partition would be a somewhat difficult maneuver.

"But this is purely mathematical conjecture and, as against that, we have the evidence of the officer, which I find is not only truthful but also well recollected, and, contrary to what one might assume could not be done, he has testified what, in fact, has taken place. I'm satisfied that the evidence of the officer is correct and accurate and that he saw what he said he did."

"Justice!" shouted the defendant in a 1976 American criminal case. "I demand justice!"

"Silence!" ordered the judge. "Are you forgetting where you are?"

From time to time, lots of people — including lawyers — seem to forget where they are when they're in court. A perfect example of this phenomenon occurred in a Sonora, California, courtroom in 1988, when a defense attorney alleged that his opponent farted his way to victory in a criminal prosecution.

Following Gary Davenport's conviction on several charges of burglary, his lawyer, Clark Head, announced that he was launching an appeal because of Assistant District Attorney Ned Lowenbach's excessive flatulence.

"It was disgusting," Head declared after the four-week jury trial. "He [the prosecutor] farted about a hundred times. He even lifted his leg several times."

Head said that Lowenbach apologized once, claiming that he'd accidentally broken wind. "But," said counsel for the defense, "he just kept doing it — as if to show his disrespect for me, my case and my client. I've been through fifty jury trials, and I've never seen anything like this."

The crowning insult, Head told reporters, was when the prosecutor let several rippers during the defense's closing argument to the jury.

"The closing argument is supposed to be sort of sacred," he said. "It's like the defendant's last chance and you aren't supposed to interrupt it. Certainly not by farting and making the jury laugh."

Head alleged that his opponent also repeatedly "moved around and ripped pages of paper" throughout the long trial. "And then he'd fart again," he said. "It was impossible to concentrate."

Distracting a jury is one of the oldest tricks in the book, usually pulled by a lawyer who has a very weak case. If he's in such a jackpot, the lawyer doesn't want the jurors to realize just how strong his opponent's case is — and how wobbly is his own. If he can somehow break their concentration, the full impact of the dreaded evidence won't register on the jurors' minds and he might still be in the running.

And that reminds me of the classic case of Jim Maddin and the fire bells.

James William Maddin, K.C., was one of the most brilliant criminal lawyers Canada has ever produced — a fun-loving, hell-raising counsel who used every trick he could to win his cases. He practiced law in Springhill, Nova Scotia, from 1900 to 1902, and in the small city of Sydney, Nova Scotia, from 1902 to 1944, when he became a magistrate. In his years at the bar, he defended sixty men charged with murder, and only two of them went to the gallows.

Maddin won his first two murder cases, but in 1904, when he defended a chap named Jack MacRae who was charged with murdering his father, it seemed his record was going to slip to two and one. Maddin thought that the old doctrine that an accused person was innocent until proven guilty was receiving too strict an interpretation in the MacRae case. He feared that the judge, and some of the jurors, considered the accused must be guilty or he wouldn't be on trial.

As the trial progressed, the Crown's case became stronger. Maddin needed a gimmick — something that would divert the jurors' minds from the evidence.

Finally, he got something he could latch onto. The sound of fire bells, located less than a block away, floated through the open window in the Sydney courthouse. Maddin counted the number of rings, which designated in which ward the fire was burning.

"My Lord," he said to the judge, "there appears to be a bad fire somewhere in Ward Four. Two of the jurors live in Ward Four. I suggest that you adjourn this trial for a while to permit them to see if their homes and families are safe."

"Mr. Maddin," said the judge sternly, "please proceed with the case! And do not interrupt this trial again!"

After several minutes, the fire bells rang again.

"Now it's in Ward Three, My Lord!" Maddin exclaimed. "There's a juror here from Ward Three and I'm sure he's concerned about his home and family!"

Once again, Maddin was reprimanded by the bench — in stronger terms than before.

The trial proceeded smoothly for a short while, and then Maddin became fascinated with the flapping of the blinds in the high-windowed court. He was on his feet again.

"My Lord," he announced, "I notice there's been a change in the direction of the wind." He said this might carry the flames toward two other wards and he mentioned the names of several other jurors who might be concerned.

The judge blasted him again.

By this time the jury's attention was pretty well centered on the defense counsel, who'd weathered three run-ins with the judge and somehow escaped being cited for contempt of court. From then on, the jurors began to pay more attention to Maddin and the defense of accident that he was putting forward.

In his closing address, Maddin convinced the jurors that the fatality was accidental, and they took less than two hours to return a verdict of not guilty. Later, out of gratitude for his efforts, Jack MacRae named a son after Maddin.

Every now and then, all hell breaks loose in court and folks who are mighty riled up kind of forget themselves for a moment or three and, yes, they employ naughty language. Sometimes, it's true, they indulge in *very* naughty language. But that's also the way it is outside the halls of justice. Life is life, wherever you find it.

Feelings are often super-charged in the courtroom, so it shouldn't be surprising that from time to time someone throws propriety to the winds and, linguistically, just lets 'er rip. The result is often so outrageous that it's funny.

On July 20, 1974, a man named Stanley Burhach made a brief but highly memorable appearance in Provincial Court in Vancouver. He was charged with trespassing. On the bench was Judge Nicholas Mussallem, a former criminal lawyer who was known far and wide as a no-nonsense sort of guy.

A transcript of Burhach's quick visit to court — a classic document that's been doing the rounds since the day in question — reads as follows:

CROWN: I'll call number six on Your Honor's list, Stanley Burhach.

JUDGE: Number, which, ma'am?

CROWN: Number six, Your Honor, Stanley Burhach.

JUDGE: Six

This is another one of these. Mr. Burhach, how do you pronounce your name, sir?

ACCUSED: Burhach, B-U-R-H-A-C-H.

JUDGE: Is this trespassing on CPR property?

CROWN: National Harbors Board. On this particular matter, Your Honor, I wonder if I can ask the accused whether or not he has seen Doctor Croft.

JUDGE: If he hasn't, he's certainly going to.

CLERK: He appeared yesterday in Court Three, Your Honor. He was put over to today to allow him to — Judge McCarthy put it over to today to allow him to see Doctor — a doctor. A request was made that he see the doctor. I imagine — I haven't been able, myself, to confirm whether or not he did see the —

JUDGE: Well, he —

CLERK: — doctor.

JUDGE: — doesn't look well to me. Look, constable, he seems sick and underfed. I'm going to put him over to Monday morning.

CROWN: Thank you, Your Honor.

JUDGE: Now, I'm doing that in his interest.

ACCUSED: But I'm sick steady for forty years — cock-sucking.

COURT OFFICER: Hey!

ACCUSED: Fuck you!

JUDGE: And the same to you, sir! Well, that brought him to life.

CROWN: Is that correct, the court has remanded him to Monday in Courtroom Three?

9

JUDGE: There you are, you see? Yes, Monday morning, let Judge McCarthy have him.

CROWN: I'll call number thirty—

JUDGE: And send a report of this to the Honorable, the Attorney-General, and add "Fuck him" at the end of it, will you?

An Australian lady recently sent me a transcript that's been the cause of a great deal of laughter Down Under — a document she describes as "probably unique."

On May 5, 1986, one Yusuf Biyikli was arraigned in the Central District Criminal Court in Adelaide, South Australia, on two charges of "assault occasioning actual bodily harm."

The transcript reveals that His Honor Judge Grubb presided and Mr. Smart appeared for the Crown. The prisoner was unrepresented. As further background, I'm advised, and verily believe, that a "poofter" is a homosexual.

Now, without further ado, here's the verbatim account of Mr. Biyikli's sojourn in court:

The Queen versus Yusuf Biyikli

While the charge is being read, the following is said by the prisoner:
Shut up, fucking poofter. You poofter, thank you.

HIS HONOR: You just keep quiet. We will have a word with you in a moment.

PRISONER: Fuck to you. All right, you poofter. All right, I fuck you. That is answer.

HIS HONOR: You understand—

PRISONER: Yes, I fuck you, too. Stuff that. Fuck the Queen, fuck Australia, fuck America, all right.

HIS HONOR: It is said that you assaulted—

PRISONER: Fuck the English, America, fuck the colony, all right.

HIS HONOR: If you don't shut up—

PRISONER: Fuck the judge, too. That is not true.

HIS HONOR: Do we assume this is a plea of not guilty?

MR. SMART: Yes, I think we can assume that.

Plea: Not Guilty.

PRISONER ARRAIGNED ON SECOND CHARGE

PRISONER: I fuck you, answer you, stuff you poofter. Is that enough answer for you?

HIS HONOR: That is no answer, but I take it, it is a plea of not guilty. In view of the outrageous outburst from the accused, I assume that the torrent of language from him is a plea of not guilty to each count. Remanded for trial. Has someone been imprudent enough to grant a bail agreement?

MR. SMART: I hesitate to ask him.

PRISONER: Fuck you.

HIS HONOR: You have a very limited vocabulary. It is unfortunate. Perhaps you would do better in your own language. Do you wish to ask for bail?

PRISONER: You ask yourself bail. Now ask me.

HIS HONOR: I don't have to ask —

PRISONER: Fuck the bail, fuck Australia.

HIS HONOR: I take it, then, you don't wish to seek bail.

PRISONER: Stuff that.

HIS HONOR: No application for bail. The accused is remanded for trial in custody.

PRISONER: Fucking bastard, poofter.

ACCUSED REMANDED IN CUSTODY FOR TRIAL

Provincial Court Judge Pat Curran of Halifax tells of a chap who was much more subtle than Mr. Biyikli when it came to expressing himself.

A few years ago, Judge Curran ran into an old friend, a Provincial Court judge from a Western province who took great delight in telling a story on himself. He'll be referred to herein as "Mike."

"Mike was presiding at an arraignment day," Judge Curran reports. "One of the parade of alleged offenders had been charged with causing a disturbance. When the accused came forward, he was wearing a T-shirt with this inscription on the front:

FIRST
UNITED
CHURCH OF
KENORA

"Mike said he immediately thought to himself, 'The nerve of this character, thinking he can sway my decision by presenting a religious connection before me.'

"When court was over for the morning, the clerk asked Mike if he had noticed the man with the T-shirt. Mike said, 'Yeah! The nerve of that fellow, trying to use religion to get himself off!'

"'Religion?' the clerk said. 'You were supposed to read the first line of the inscription *down*, not across!'

"Obviously, Mike doesn't do crossword puzzles."

A British Columbia man, who wishes to remain anonymous, sent me the next story. He knows the central character and doesn't want to embarrass him, so that fellow also gets a made-up name — Albert. My correspondent tells the tale:

"Albert was making lunch in his shack on the Indian reserve when there was a frightening squeal of tires and then a crash like an explosion, followed by yells of anger and screams of pain. He rushed out and found that two cars had collided head-on and several people were quite badly injured.

"After doing his best to help, Albert drove into the nearby village to call the police and an ambulance, and soon the injured were cared for. The cars were very badly damaged.

"Some weeks later, an inquiry was held at the local courthouse, and Albert was summoned to appear as a witness. This was a new role for him. It was not his first visit to the courthouse, but it was the first time he had gone in by the front door.

"Albert arrived with a fresh haircut and wearing a new suit, and he was impressed by all the courtesy he received from the lawyers and others. In due course he was called to the witness box, and the judge welcomed him, put him at his ease, and then explained the situation.

"'We are trying to find out exactly what happened, and why it happened,'" said the judge. 'Now please tell us what you saw.'

"This request was not quite what Albert had expected, and his carefully prepared report now seemed somewhat irrelevant. After a little hesitation, he stammered, 'Your Honor, I didn't *see* anything. I was inside my house when the crash occurred, and when I ran outside people were lying all over the place and hollering.'

"The judge persisted.

"'But didn't you see the cars collide?'

"'No, sir.'

"'Well, thank you for coming, but we have to hear from people who saw the accident happen so that I can try to determine the cause. You're welcome to stay, if you wish. Make yourself comfortable and we'll proceed with the next witness.'

"Albert's day was ruined. He sat down, shaken and a little sullen. Soon he began to doze, perhaps because of the overheated room, or possibly from all the excitement.

"Then suddenly there was a very audible 'social accident,' followed by a minor panic as people nearby scrambled to escape into a more salubrious atmosphere. The judge, trying hard to keep his composure, thumped on his desk and called for order. He had some scathing remarks for Albert and told a constable to escort him outside.

"Just as the door was opening, Albert turned around and asked loudly: 'Your Honor, did you see it, or did you only hear it?'"

Albert was quite fortunate, really. His was only a *little* "social accident." Barrie, Ontario, lawyer Kevin Carroll, Q.C., recollects — not so fondly — the day a miscalculating court reporter had a *major* mishap. We're talking here, folks, about a fellow who turned the other cheek and, in so doing, literally stunk out the joint.

"It was during a Supreme Court of Ontario trial in Barrie," Kevin recalls with scrunched-up nose. "While I was examining a witness, there was, suddenly, this *terrible, terrible* smell that had everyone practically gagging. It got worse and worse until it was unbearable and the judge announced a fifteen-minute recess.

"As soon as His Lordship had disappeared from view, I sighed and said, 'Thank God!' The court reporter looked up from his notebook and said, 'It's "Thank God!" for *you*, but what about *me*?'"

Says Kevin, who always had a way with words, "The reporter had shit himself!"

√ Fred W. Barry practiced law in Kimberley, British Columbia, from 1946 until his retirement in 1977. Fred had a spaniel that he loved dearly — a Brittany pointer named "Footy" — and for years Footy followed Fred from one courthouse to another.

"I did a lot of trial work," Fred told me recently, "and Footy often came into court with me. He was no trouble to anyone. He'd lie down under the counsel table and wouldn't stir. He just wanted to be with his master."

Because he was so well behaved, most judges didn't mind if Footy attended the proceedings — even jury trials. But, says Fred, there was one judge who hated dogs — in or out of the courtroom — and the last time Fred Barry appeared in that judge's court, His Honor had Footy evicted.

But a few minutes later, when someone entered the courtroom, Footy trotted back in behind him. The delighted spectators nearly burst into applause.

A short time later, Fred Barry sold his practice and called it a day. Footy, alas, had visited his last courtroom. A lot of people thought that was a shame, seeing as Footy was so fond of hanging around courthouses and other legal establishments. They wondered whether there might be some way to remedy the situation.

At a farewell supper thrown by his colleagues, Fred was presented with a fancy embossed certificate that he says he'll cherish forever.

The certificate was actually for Footy, not Fred, and it was from the Law Society of British Columbia. All but one of the benchers (governors) of the Law Society had voted in favor of it, and it was as official as any similar document ever issued to a lawyer.

Signed by the secretary and the treasurer of the Law Society, and bearing the big red seal of that august body, the document reads as follows:

"This is to Certify that Footy of Kimberley B.C. was, by the Benchers of The Law Society of British Columbia, on Tuesday the Tenth day of May, A.D. 1977, duly called to the Bar of the Province of British Columbia and admitted as a Solicitor of the Supreme

Court of British Columbia, and that at the date hereof is a member of the Society in good standing. Dated this 10th day of May A.D. 1977."

Footy died before he got much mileage out of his call to the bar. He's buried in Fred Barry's backyard and his framed certificate hangs proudly in a prominent place in Fred's home.

You never know what will pop up — or drop down — in court.

Arthur W. MacLeod Rogers, Q.C., of Victoria, British Columbia, became a lawyer way back yonder in 1921. He tells of a close call he had in court many years ago:

"I was arguing a case before the Appellate Division of the Supreme Court of Ontario when down from the huge chandelier that used to hang from the ceiling there descended on a thin filament of web a spider with a body as big as my thumb — a black widow whose bite was reputedly poisonous!

"As a boy I'd read a yarn about huge, hairy, man-eating spiders. I had bad dreams about them. So I was scared, more frightened than I'd ever been in the infantry in World War I. If the thing had landed on my face, I'd have gone crazy and stayed that way.

"I didn't swat it for fear the court would wonder what was the matter with me. I kept on talking, but couldn't have made sense. Eventually, after what seemed like a year, the spider dropped to the floor and I breathed a great sigh of relief."

And you also never know what kind of people you'll meet in and around a courtroom.

A Mississippi lawyer represented two men one afternoon on separate "lunacy commitment hearings" — inquiries as to whether a person should be admitted to a mental institution.

The first man insisted he was the president of the United States and declared that he'd have the judge and lawyers put in jail if he were put in a psychiatric hospital.

After the first hearing was over, the second man was brought in and questioned about his perception of time, place, and reality.

When he was asked if he knew who the president of the United States was, he replied: "I can't recall the fellow's name, but I just met him out there in the hall."

Sydney, Nova Scotia, lawyer David N. Muise is a great storyteller. I taped him one night when he was in full flight, relating one funny yarn after another. Here he is, giving the background of a case that was heard down his way:

"Saddie and her boyfriend came into Sydney one Friday afternoon and Judge Charlie O'Connell married them about 4:00 P.M. Saddie's uncle was with them and they used him as one of the witnesses.

"After the wedding, the three of them went to a tavern in Sydney River and got drunk, and then they went to the liquor store and got a load of booze. The bride was too drunk to sing, so she had to drive. The car was stopped by the Mounties and the bride was charged with impaired driving.

"On Monday morning, at nine-thirty, Saddie appeared before Judge O'Connell — the same judge who'd married them late Friday afternoon. Charlie kept saying, all through the trial, 'Haven't I seen you two recently?'"

On the other side of the country, in Vancouver, I taped well-known criminal lawyer Sidney B. ("Slippery Sid") Simons as he reminisced about some of his cases. Here's one of the yarns he spun:

"I was acting for a guy who was being tried in a building where they had a difficult security situation. There was just a lock-up room in the corridor behind the courtroom, where the judges walked back and forth, and so when the matter began they brought the client in from the lock-up and had him sitting in the front row in the courtroom as evidence was being heard.

"Lunch break came and everyone dispersed with the usual haste, and since they weren't used to having people in custody there, I guess they forgot about this man. And everybody left and he was all alone in the courtroom.

"It was lunch time, so he decided there was no use hanging around there, so he left, got on a bus, went home, showered, shaved, cleaned up, changed his clothes, and came back for the afternoon sitting.

"Everyone was in a panic because they realized there was a prisoner gone. Someone had screwed up and hadn't taken him back to the lock-up.

"I came back in just moments before the case was to resume and I saw the guy sitting there; meanwhile, everyone was saying, 'Your client's disappeared — he's escaped!' I said, 'No, no, he's right *there*.'

"So everyone calmed down a bit and Judge Les Bewley came into the courtroom. We didn't finish the trial that day and I asked the judge if he'd consider releasing my client. 'He's been in custody for a couple of months and can't raise bail,' I told him. 'He's got no money.'

"Judge Bewley wanted to know what happened when my client was at large earlier that day. I explained to him that he'd gone home and cleaned up and come back. He said, 'All right, young fellow, how much money do you have in your pocket?' The client replied, 'I spent most of it on the bus. I've got ten cents left.' And the judge said, 'Okay, that's your bail. You're remanded with bail until the next court date.'"

Harvey G. Walker, a lawyer in North Battleford, Saskatchewan, recalls a case in which a man accused of an offense said he pleaded not guilty so he could "get in my two cents worth." Provincial Court Judge Joseph Policha found the man guilty and fined him two cents.

"The decision and penalty were widely reported in the press," Harvey states. "However, the best part of the story was missed. The accused failed to pay his fine and the judge paid it himself."

In 1988, in Whitehorse, Yukon Territory, a man admitted he was guilty of mischief. He smashed a window in a "bathroom brawl" that began when he refused to smoke a marijuana joint proffered by two others in the room. The others then became abusive.

As the accused tried to push his way out of the room, his hand went through a small window in the bathroom door. He later paid thirty-two dollars to repair the window. He also apologized to the court for his actions.

Judge Lynch Staunton felt that the others were more to blame than the accused and so he imposed a fine of only one dollar — payable over the next one thousand years.

The late Mr. Justice Stuart Purvis, of the Court of Queen's Bench of Alberta, wrote to me about prairie justice in earlier — and simpler — times:

"When I was a teenager in the small village of Viking, ninety miles east of Edmonton, Chief Judge Lucien Dubuc of the Alberta District Court presided over court on a regular basis in the village library. The sessions proved to be popular entertainment and the characters involved always played to a full house.

"On one occasion, in the late 1930s, my father, a lawyer, was defending an alleged horse thief. About halfway through the proceedings, Chief Judge Dubuc interrupted with the inquiry: 'Mr. Purvis, where is your client?'

"Much to the mortification of defense counsel and six-foot-four Corporal 'Tiny' Bain of the Royal Canadian Mounted Police, the accused had disappeared!

"After a frantic search, the police surrounded the outhouse at the back of the library building and apprehended the miscreant as he emerged after having unobtrusively and innocently answered a call of nature.

"The Mounties always get their man!"

And, speaking of earlier times, here's a true story about the bad old days:

A few years ago, a plaque honoring a ravenous rascal named Packer, for whom a Washington cafeteria was named, was removed from the wall of the eatery because it was considered to be in bad taste. You see, Alferd Packer was convicted in 1874 of killing and eating five gold prospectors he'd been hired to guide through the Rocky Mountains.

On sentencing the scoundrel, the judge made the following remarks:

"There was only six Demycrats in all of Hinsdale County and you, you man-eating son of a bitch, ate five of them! I sentence you to hang, to hang until you're dead, dead, dead, as a warning agin further reducin' this county's Demycratic population!"

√ Moving ahead to much more recent times, here's an amusin' but confusin' chunk of dialogue from an American courtroom:

Q. Where was she?

A. In the living room.

Q. Is that where you placed her under arrest also?

A. Yes.

Q. Did you then unarrest the defendant?

A. Yes.

Q. How did you communicate that to her?

A. I told her she wasn't under arrest no more.

Q. And then did you arrest her again?

A. Yes.

Q. Then did you unarrest her again?

A. Yes.

Q. When did the second unarrest take place?

A. When the captain told me I was going to be reprimanded.

Q. For arresting her or unarresting her?

A. No, arresting her.

Q. So you arrested the lady, the captain told you to unarrest her, and the captain told you you would be reprimanded for arresting her, then you arrested her again?

A. I arrested her, the captain told me to unarrest her, and knowing that the captain was wrong I arrested her again, then he told me, "Well, you'd better unarrest her." And I unarrested her.

Vancouver lawyer Terry La Liberté tells about a colleague, Henry Brown, who was retained in a criminal case by a fellow who was not very fast on the uptake.

When the court clerk called out the name of his client, shortly after eleven o'clock in the morning, Brown stepped forward and said a few words to the judge about the case. Then the judge, anxious to have some java, said: "I'm going to stand down court for twenty minutes."

Whereupon the client shook his lawyer's hand and said, "Gee, Mr. Brown, you're fantastic! I thought I'd get at least thirty days!"

Angel Guerra is director of marketing at Stoddart Publishing, the folks who publish my books on courtroom humor. For quite some time I've been telling Angel that the courts are full of humor and that you never know when somebody is going to say or do something funny therein.

Well, now he knows first-hand that I wasn't giving him any phoney baloney. Recently Angel went to Provincial Court in Toronto to testify as a witness. As always, there were many people facing trial — one of them a man whose surname was "Innocent."

When the judge entered the courtroom, he scanned the docket, smiled at something he'd just seen, glanced up and said to no one in particular: "Which one of you is Innocent?"

"Immediately," Angel reports, "ten or twelve guys stood up and said, 'I am!'"

Mr. Justice George L. Murray, of the Supreme Court of British Columbia, told me about a celebrated case from yesteryear.

Back in the 1950s and 1960s, before Legal Aid came on the scene, it was fairly common for persons serving prison terms to file and argue their own appeals.

One day, a number of prisoners were transported from jail to the swanky digs of the Court of Appeal. As each name on the appeal list was called, that person was sworn in and then told the judges why he thought he shouldn't have been convicted or should have received a lighter sentence. Included on that list was the name MacKenzie George.

When the name MacKenzie George was called, a prison guard practically shoved an Indian man into the witness box.

After the fellow had been sworn in, one of the judges leaned forward and said, "Now, MacKenzie George, what have you got to say?"

"Nothing!" said the man in the box.

"Nothing?" said the judge. "Nothing? Now, look here, the government has gone to great expense to bring you here today, and Crown Counsel has no doubt worked hard to prepare his case for argument. You're the one who wanted the appeal, and now you inform the court that you have nothing to say! MacKenzie George, *why* do you have nothing to say?"

"Because," the man replied, "I'm not MacKenzie George!"

2

TAKE THE WITNESS — PLEASE!

IF NOBODY EVER SAID ANYTHING UNLESS HE KNEW
WHAT HE WAS TALKING ABOUT, WHAT A GHASTLY HUSH
WOULD DESCEND UPON THE EARTH.

A. P. Herbert

Our courts would shut down lickety-split if they experienced a hush, ghastly or otherwise, for the fuel that keeps them going — for ever and ever — is the good old-fashioned, indispensable, spoken word. Billions and trillions and zillions of spoken words, to be real precise about the matter.

Prosecutions and lawsuits must be proven with the sworn testimony of people who go into the witness box and state what they saw and heard. They are then questioned by lawyers who "test" their evidence this way and that, and now and then the judge chimes in, too. This all takes time — often gobs of time — so the witness box isn't the best place to be for folks who are in a hurry.

But most witnesses *are* in a hurry — to get the hell out of the uncomfortable, intimidating atmosphere of the courtroom and back to their usual haunts. Through nervousness or stupidity — or both — they sometimes blurt out words that cause listeners to cackle with glee. This is great, at least for the cacklers, for it's a scientific fact that mirth and merriment promote mental and physical health.

So let's toast such benefactors, whether they're funny accidentally or on purpose, and then let's take a squint at what some of them have been saying of late.

A lot of witnesses, when asked a very simple question, become instant comedians. For example, in an assault case there was this zippy exchange:

JUDGE: Can you describe the defendant?
COMPLAINANT: That's what I was doing when he hit me.

Saskatoon lawyer Grant Currie captured some memorable dialogue, which reads as follows:

Q. How long have you lived in Prince Albert?
A. All my life except maybe three years when I was twelve.

London, Ontario, court reporter Gail McGilvray mined this gem:

Q. Where were you born?
A. I was born in Nova Scotia, originally.

Sandra Spicer, a court reporter in Grande Prairie, Alberta, preserved the following for posterity:

Q. And this all happened in Valleyview in the Province of Alberta?
A. Oh, no, I was born in Indianhead, Saskatchewan.

This compulsion to fire off zingers is epidemic, it appears. In the spirit of free trade, which is all the rage these days, I submit herewith a smattering of one-liners from south of the world's longest undefended border:

• Q. Your residence?
  A. Columbus, Ohio.
  Q. And, length of residence?

A. Forty-eight feet, seven inches — not including the porch.

• Q. Where do you live?
A. At home.
Q. How long have you lived there?
A. ~~All my life.~~ *Since I moved.*

• Q. Where do you live?
A. I moved.

• Q. Ma'am, how long have you lived in this town?
A. All my life.
Q. And how old are you?
A. Thirty.
Q. How long have you been thirty?
A. Quite a while.

• Q. Is that a permanent address?
A. No, sir, it's a house.

• Q. What is your marital status?
A. Right now, it's not too good.

• Q. What are your hobbies?
A. Drinking coffee and watching girls.

• Q. Who was your lawyer on that case?
A. A little old Italian named Schwartz.

• Q. Tell what happened to the judge.
A. Why, did something happen to the judge?

• Q. When was your last visit to Dr. Allenby?
A. I'll have to guess March or April.
Q. What was he doing to you?
A. He was trying to determine a reason that I couldn't maintain an erection.
Q. Do you have any plans to see him again?

A. Nothing firm, no.

A few years ago, Mark Hornblower, an Assistant Crown Attorney in Sarnia, Ontario, prosecuted a fellow on a charge of careless driving.

"The accused was asked two simple questions that warranted two simple one-word answers," Mark says. "To the question as to the amount of beer he'd had, the answer is three. As to whether he felt the effects of it, the answer is no."

But . . . well, let's look at the transcript of what was said:

Q. How many beer would you say you had?
A. I had bought six tickets and I bought, and I met up with some dudes that I knew there and I drank two in the afternoon, like this was, I got there about five o'clock and I drank two then and I bought a buddy of mine, like two guys that I'd met there, one of them happened to be in the car that I hit, I guess, but didn't know that until weeks after, but anyway. And, I still had a ticket in my pocket, so I had three beers from about five o'clock in the afternoon until the time of the accident.
Q. So you had three beers.
A. Yeah, I had some, I had some coffee too, cause I was getting hungry, that's why I was on my way to the, to the, like I drank them in the afternoon when I first got there, but I didn't feel like, it was a hot day, that's why I drank them and then I didn't feel like it after that, like I was on the motorcycle and you know.
Q. Were you feeling any effects of the beer?
A. No, well, like I say I had coffee. I had been talking to a bunch of people, they'd all talked to me out there and everybody I talked to, my memory is a little, like on some of it, is, but the people that I've talked to, you know, since, like I was talking to people out there and they said, what happened to you, you know, like, you weren't, when I was talking to you when you were, you know, you weren't, like what happened, you know. So, like, I wasn't, no, I don't think I was feeling any effects from the alcohol.

Now that that's all cleared up, let's eavesdrop on another articulate chap:

Q. The deposition is a question-and-answer session, which we've already started. I asked you a few questions, and you answered them.

A. Uh-huh.

Q. It's the same basic procedure that we will follow until I've asked you all the questions that I have for you.

A. Uh-huh.

Q. We're going to get along much better, and the court reporter will be much happier, if you will try not to make any sounds or partial responses when I'm talking. You do have a tendency to do that. And when you interject a "yes" or an "uh-huh" —

A. Uh-huh.

Q. — the court reporter has the burden — you just did it again —

A. Uh-huh.

Q. — of trying to take down all of the questions and sounds that you are making when she also has to take down what I'm saying. You will make her job much easier today if you will be so kind as not to say anything until I finish a question. I will then wait for your complete —

A. Uh-huh.

Q. — answer. You just did it again!

A. Uh-huh.

Q. Before I —

A. Uh-huh.

Q. — ask you a question, I'll wait for your full response. With only one person talking at a time, everything will go just fine. When we both talk at the same time, life is very difficult for her. Will you do that?

A. Yep.

Q. Please answer out loud in full words rather than with a nod or a grunt because —

A. Yes.

Q. You just interrupted!

The next witness is no prize, either:

Q. Where were you when you first assumed there would be a collision?
A. Hard to say.
Q. Were you out of the intersection?
A. It's hard to say.
Q. Do you know?
A. Do I know what?
Q. Whether or not you were in or out of the intersection.
A. When what?

This bloke was a big help, too:

Q. Do you suffer from any specifically diagnosed medical condition like Alzheimer's disease or anything that would specifically contribute to the hampering of your memory?
A. Not that I remember.

A crisper version of the foregoing comes from a trial in Canada's Northwest Territories:

Q. Do you have any problems with your memory?
A. Not that I can recall.

And in the Yukon Territory, it appears, folks are just as stingy with their words as they are in the neighboring N.W.T. In a recent trial in Whitehorse, the judge was questioning a ten-year-old girl before deciding whether or not she should be sworn in. Court reporter Sharon Gateley preserved this short-winded exchange:

Q. Now, do you know the difference between telling the truth and telling a lie?
A. Yeah.
Q. How did you find that out?
A. By Hughie.
Q. By who?
A. By Hugh.

Q. By?
A. Hugh.
Q. Here?
A. Hugh.
Q. By me?
A. No.
CROWN ATTORNEY H. F. K. CONNOLLY: By Hugh, My Lord.
THE COURT: By Hugh?
MR. CONNOLLY: That's my first name.
THE COURT: I see.
THE COURT: You call him Hugh, eh?

Every child of "tender years" who's brought forward as a poten-
tial witness is quizzed about the importance of telling the truth.
It must be shown that the youngster believes that he or she can,
in some way, be punished for lying. Otherwise, the evidence
can't be taken under oath — which is another way of saying it's
not worth a damn. When this happens, the trial might very well
skid to a halt.

But if a kiddie is welcomed into the witness box, watch out!
Children can blow you away with a devastating weapon called
honesty — blatant, unabashed honesty. You see, a great many
small-fry who testify haven't yet learned how to fib. These are
uncomplicated and undevious little people who look you in the
eye and tattoo you with the truth. The squad that has such a tyke
on its roster often wins the case.

Also, kids who habitually blurt out the truth sometimes say
funny things. This, too, is a bonus, because laughter loosens
you up, and if you're loose you might triumph. (Then again,
you might not — but at least you've had a better time than the
other guys.)

And another thing — pint-sized witnesses are often technical
as hell. For example:

Q. Now, Gary, all your responses must be oral. Okay?
A. Oral.
Q. How old are you?
A. Oral.

In another case, in which the court reporter said she was having trouble catching some of a child's responses, we have the following dialogue:

Q. Depending on whether there was any problems?
A. Uh-huh.
Q. You have to say yes for her.
A. Yes for her.
Q. Do you understand what I'm saying? Your nods don't show up on the record. You have to say yes for her.
A. Yes for her.

√ In the early 1960s, a British Columbia magistrate asked a seven-year-old boy what would happen if he lied under oath, and the lad replied: "I will either go to Hell, or, if the Lord sees fit, perhaps just to Purgatory."

The boy was sworn in and he gave evidence on behalf of the Crown. On cross-examination, defense counsel tried to show that the witness was an over-imaginative little fellow:
"Tommy, have you got a dog?"
"Yes."
"Does the dog talk to you at times?"
"Now, you know a dog can't talk."
The lawyer shifted gears.
"Have you ever seen a fairy?"
"Yes."
"Well, what was the fairy doing?"
"It was waiting to take passengers across the Fraser River."

√ Some adult witnesses can be pretty technical, too. In a U.S. motor-vehicle accident case, the defendant was asked, "Please state the location of your right foot immediately prior to the impact."

"Immediately before the impact," the man replied, "my right foot was located at the immediate end of my right leg."

√ And then there's the cautious witness, the citizen who picks his or her words ever so carefully. In a British case, a number of valuable homing pigeons had been shot. The witness, a farmer, was the owner of the pigeons.

"Are you prepared to swear on your oath that my client shot your pigeons?" defense counsel asked the nervous witness.

"I didn't say he shot them," the man replied. "I just said I suspected him of doing so."

"Now we're getting to it!" the lawyer declared. "What made you suspect my client?"

"Well," said the farmer, "first, I caught him on my land with a gun. Second, I heard a gun go off and heard some pigeons fall. Third, I found four of my pigeons in his pocket — and I don't think them birds flew there and shot themselves."

In an Edmonton lawsuit, court reporter Doreen Johnson took down some evidence that belongs on TV's "Wild Kingdom." It goes as follows:

Q. During the time you lived on the homestead, did your husband have any livestock?

A. No, we didn't have any. First, we had a cat, and then we had a dog. Then somebody gave us two chickens with little chicklets and the chicken hawk ate all the chicklets and the dog ate the chicken.

Judge F. S. Fisher, of the Ontario Provincial Court (Family Division), recently heard a case in which a wife sought permission to serve legal documents on her mother-in-law, rather than on her husband, the intended recipient. She said her husband was hiding out in his mother's home and was obviously evading service. If the papers were served on her mother-in-law, she said, they would surely be brought to her husband's attention.

To grant such an order, the judge would have to be satisfied that the husband was, in fact, living at his mother's place. So he probed into the matter, as follows:

JUDGE: How do you know your husband lives with his mother?

WIFE: Because he phones me from her place.

JUDGE: How do you know it's her place he's phoning from?

WIFE: Because his mother has a bird called Daisy. Daisy has a habit of nibbling on the phone wire when someone's on the phone.

JUDGE: Yes?

WIFE: When he phones me, Daisy nibbles on the wire, my husband gets mad, swears and whacks at the bird, and then the bird squawks and so I know he's at his mother's.

JUDGE: Application granted.

Edmonton court reporter Chris Brower captured this amusin' but confusin' testimony:

A. There was one guy that came up and sat with us. Harvey knew him, but I didn't know him.

Q. Harvey Newman?

A. No, Harvey knew him, but I didn't know him.

The next few witnesses kind of leave you wondering, "Huh?"

- Q You have a daughter named Walter?
  A Walter.
  Q. And what is your son's name?
  A Pearl.

- Q. About what age man would you guess him to be?
  A. You got me there. I'm poor at guessing ages, because I'm forty-six myself.

- Q. When were you first aware, after the collision, that you had been injured?
  A. Well, as soon as my head hit the pavement, I knew I was unconscious.

- Q. Do you know how tall your husband is?
  A. Yes, I know exactly. We measured each other last week, and he's either five feet eleven or eleven feet five.

"I searched the prisoner and found nothing on him," a policeman testified in an Irish court. "It was afterwards handed back to him."

"The man was speechless drunk," another Irish witness said under oath.
    "How do you know he was speechless?" asked the magistrate.
    "I could tell by his voice," the witness replied.

This sort of discombobulated discourse — sometimes called "speaking Irish" — is heard frequently in the courts of Ireland. Here's another example:

A He fell on the road several times. He was so drunk that he couldn't keep his feet.
Q. If he was so drunk, how was he able to run after you?
A. He followed after me between falling and rising.

How's this for conclusive evidence? Said an Irish witness to the magistrate: "He was sober enough to know he was drunk."

As everyone knows, Irishmen love to fight. I was reminded of this recently when I came across a report of a court case in which a Dublin man asked a magistrate to impose a peace bond against his three sons. He wasn't as hard on his youngest offspring as he was on the others.
    "Patrick is the only one of me boys who ever showed me any rale affection," the father told the court, "for he never struck me when I was down."

When folks testify in court, their words don't always come out the way they were meant to.
    Mr. Justice M. E. Shannon, of the Court of Queen's Bench of Alberta, recalls a case in which a Calgary man sought a divorce on the grounds of his wife's cruelty. His Lordship records for posterity this courtroom exchange between lawyer and client:

Q. What did your wife do to you?
A. She abused me verbally and called me a lot of bad names.

Q. Are you separated now?

A. Yes, we've been separated for three weeks.

Q. And how have things been going since you've separated?

A. Things are much better now. With my wife gone, I'm feeling myself again.

In another divorce case, heard in Moncton, New Brunswick, a woman alleged that her husband had been mentally cruel by calling a halt to sexual relations.

"Isn't it true that you refused to have sex with your wife?" the woman's lawyer asked the husband on cross-examination.

"No, that's not true at all," the man replied.

After a brief confab between lawyer and client, the questioning continued.

"You refused to have oral sex, isn't that correct?"

"*That*, yes."

"Why?"

"Because I'm a vegetarian."

Roy A. Yerex is a Winnipeg lawyer, but I suspect that in an earlier life he was a private eye, or a mystery writer, or maybe both. In a recent letter to me, Roy related a heart-tugging tale about a damsel in distress. Here it is, in the author's inimitable style:

"She came to me for help. She was from Quebec — beautiful, alluring in her aloneness, in desperate flight from an abusive brute of a husband who mistook her for a punching bag and her child for a pawn in his battle for supremacy in the marriage. Could I do anything?

"Could I do anything for a lady in distress, lately from Quebec, barely able to speak or understand English, with liquid brown eyes that pleaded for protection? What Western Canadian male lawyer with a precedent for an order to prohibit an alcoholic husband from 'molesting, annoying or harassing' such a vulnerable creature couldn't?

"Off to the Family Court with motion in hand and client in tow to give evidence damning the monster who would take advantage of such a delicate creature.

"Like a well-oiled machine, the proceedings purred to the granting of the order forbidding the husband to 'molest, annoy or harass' her, in spite of the fact that she had problems with every sentence she had to speak or hear in English.

"Outside the court, beaming with triumph, I stood, like a white knight dismounted from his white charger, to modestly accept the adoration of a client finally freed from tyranny.

" 'But,' she said in halting English, 'I'm surpise dee judge he would say such a ting.'

" 'I beg your pardon,' I replied, questioningly.

" 'You know, 'ow my 'usband, 'e can't 'ave sex wit' me.'

"A moment of slight confusion on my part and then, 'Well, he can't have sex with you, but the judge didn't specifically state that.'

" 'Pardonnez-moi, you can't say 'e din't. No judge in Quebec would say such a ting!'

"The judge had not referred to sex at all, and I asked her what she had heard that I didn't.

" 'You know, when 'e say, Mr. Yerex, you have your order dat my 'usban can't moles' or annoy my ass.'"

Another Winnipeg lawyer, Abe Anhang, also checks in with a report from the marital wars. He starts by setting the scene:

"Judge Mary Wawrykow (now deceased) was dealing for the thousandth time with the usual complaint: a woman needing more support from a husband who claimed he was not able to afford it."

When the wife's lawyer rose to cross-examine the husband, Abe says, the dialogue went as follows:

Q. I note from your list of expenses that you spend sixty-five dollars a month on taxi fares, is that correct?

A. Yes.

Q. Isn't it true that you work as a bus driver for the Transit Commission?

A. Yes.

JUDGE (*intervening*): I've had many bus drivers here before and I know that you fellows get free passes. Why don't you ride the bus?

A. Because I have to get to work very early. I drive one of the early buses.

JUDGE: Yes, I know, I know. Don't fool with me. There's a shuttle bus to pick up the drivers. Why don't you use the shuttle bus?

A. I'm the one who *drives* the shuttle bus.

Claresholm, Alberta, lawyer Donald J. Welbourne recollects:

"The judge called a ten-minute recess in a steamy sexual-assault trial, before the complainant had completely finished her graphic description of how the accused had ripped the clothes from her body in the back seat of a car.

"Upon court resuming, the judge, to put the complainant at ease, said nicely, 'Now where were you?'

" 'I was just in the washroom,' came the innocent reply."

Provincial Court Judge C. J. Cannon of Toronto recalls a case in which two young men were charged with robbing a convenience store. The manager of the store was a woman of Korean ancestry who spoke pretty good English. When she was asked to describe the robbers she said they were both of average size and there was nothing particularly noteworthy about either of them.

The woman was asked to take a good look around the courtroom to see if she could identify the culprits. In doing so, she looked straight through the actual robbers.

"Do you see the men who robbed you that night?" asked the Crown Attorney.

"To tell you the truth," she replied, "all Occidentals look alike to me."

As Will Shakespeare once inquired, "What's in a name?" The next couple of yarns might shed some light on the subject.

Trial lawyer Bert Raphael, Q.C., of Toronto, writes: "In Ontario, Supreme Court judges are addressed as 'My Lord' and District Court judges as 'Your Honor.'

"As I was marshaling my witness' evidence in a recent trial in the Supreme Court of Ontario, he kept responding to questions from the bench by addressing the judge as 'Your Honor.' Rather than embarrass him before the judge, I waited for an appropriate break in the proceedings and then instructed my witness to reply to the judge as 'My Lord.'

"He said he simply could not do that and when I pressed him as to why he would not follow my instructions he replied, 'Because I'm an atheist."

For as long as anyone can remember, and then some, Newfoundlanders have conferred the honorary title of "Captain" on all sorts of men who've reached their twilight years — even gents who've never gone to sea.

A Newfoundland judge who prefers to remain anonymous relates that one day, quite a while back, one such senior citizen, a confirmed landlubber, went to court to testify at a trial. Noting he'd been addressed as "Captain," the judge asked the old fellow how he rated such a moniker.

"Well, Me Honor," the witness replied, "the 'Captain' in front of me name is just like the 'Honorable' in front of yours. It don't mean a damn thing."

The Honorable Noel Goodridge, Chief Justice of Newfoundland, visits Memory Lane — and the Topsail Highway:

"Chief Justice R. S. Furlong was hearing a case involving an automobile accident on the Topsail Highway, between St. John's and Conception Bay. One of the witnesses was relating some incidents that occurred along the highway and was trying to spot them by reference to the numerous public houses along that road.

"When pressed by the Chief Justice for more accuracy, he explained that he was from another part of the province and was not very familiar with the public houses along the highway, and he concluded by saying, 'Your Lordship would be more familiar with them than I.'"

In Newfoundland, as everywhere else, it ain't easy to get some folks to cooperate with the Crown. A former Crown Attorney, Mr. Justice Seamus B. O'Regan of the Supreme Court of Newfoundland, recalls one such case:

"I was prosecuting a woman who was charged with murdering her husband. She'd spent many years 'on the street' and had a rather 'seedy' reputation. She took the stand and, basically, informed the jury that she remembered nothing of the night in question as she'd been on a 'drinking spree' at the time.

"The murder occurred on a Sunday morning and, according to her, she'd bought two bottles of 'Pinky' — a well-known local sherry — for seven dollars from a man she didn't know.

" 'I drank both of them and spent the rest of the day with "Dead Eye Taylor,"' she testified.

" 'Dead Eye,' at the time of the trial, was serving fifteen years in Dorchester Penitentiary in New Brunswick, and I arranged to have him brought to court.

"Needless to say, 'Dead Eye' turned hostile, and I was given leave to cross-examine him.

"I put the question to 'Dead Eye' as to what, if anything, he had to say about the accused buying two bottles of 'Pinky' for seven dollars, from a man she didn't know, on a Sunday morning, and drinking both of them.

"Looking the jury straight in the eye, he hesitated, thought for a while, and then replied: 'Two bottles . . . for seven dollars . . . on a Sunday morning. . . . Well, I'd say she got a bargain!'"

Halifax lawyer Donald A. Kerr, Q.C., an expert in Admiralty law, has a salty tale to tell:

"Philip J. Lewis, Q.C., a practicing lawyer until his death a few years ago in his late eighties, was unquestionably the dean of the Newfoundland bar. He told the story of a schooner captain whose vessel was run down and sunk by an American convoy on the Grand Banks on a foggy night during World War II. The skipper was summoned to Washington to testify before a U.S. Board of Naval Inquiry, and Mr. Lewis accompanied him.

"Cross-examination by the attorney for the convoy commander was hard and merciless. The skipper habitually wore, and carried to the witness box with him, a greasy old cloth cap which he kept clutched between his fists. One could tell, according to Mr. Lewis, the impact of the question by the number of twists the skipper put in the cap.

"The skipper explained how, without warning, he had suddenly found himself in the middle of the unlighted convoy, with merchantmen and destroyers zooming past him at high speed.

"'Why didn't you give those vessels some warning of your presence, before you were hit?' demanded the attorney.

" ''Ow was I suppose to do dat, sorr?' asked the skipper.

"'Why, you could have blown your fog horn or made some other kind of signal,' said the lawyer.

"'We don't have no horn, sorr,' the skipper replied.

"'Well, you do have a little cannon on your forecastle, do you not, for calling in the dories at the end of the day?'

"The skipper nodded.

"'Why didn't you fire that?'

"According to Mr. Lewis, the skipper added two twists to his cap and 'squzz it til de juice run out.'

"'If I had fired dat gun, in the middle of dat convoy, I'd be in Hell now, sorr — where *you* should be!' the skipper said with great passion.

"'Not an inappropriate comment, I think,' said the chairman. And that was the end of the cross-examination."

Ted Green, a detective sergeant with the Ontario Provincial Police, recalls a case in Sudbury in which a man pleaded guilty to a charge of having care and control of his car while impaired by alcohol.

An OPP officer advised the court that he'd seen the accused stagger out of a pub and lurch towards his vehicle. He said the man dropped his keys as he tried to unlock the door, fell as he tried to pick them up, and then managed to scramble into the car and get behind the wheel.

"When I approached the accused, he became very belligerent," the officer said, "and he kept swearing at me as I placed him under arrest."

"Are those facts substantially correct?" the judge asked the accused.

"Yes, they are, Your Honor," the man replied. "All except the part about me swearing. That's bullshit!"

In another drinking-driving case we get this snappy courtroom dialogue:

Q. Officer, do you think two years' experience as a police officer qualifies you to state definitely that this man was drunk?
A. No, sir.
Q. Upon what, then, do you base your assumption that the accused was drunk?
A. Twenty-one years of bartending.

Defense counsel must have done a bang-up job on this witness:

Q. Are you sure this is the man who stole your car last Thursday?
A. Well, I was. But now, after cross-examination, I'm not sure I ever owned a car.

We zip now to the Edmonton courthouse, where the defense lawyer in a robbery case is grilling a Crown witness.

Q. When did the robbery take place?
A. I think —
Q. We don't care what you *think*, sir. We want to know what you *know*.
A. If you don't want to know what I think, I might as well leave the stand. I can't talk without thinking. What do you think I am, a lawyer?

3

JEST A MINUTE, COUNSEL!

AGAINST THE ASSAULT OF LAUGHTER NOTHING CAN STAND.

Mark Twain

Yóu're right on the mark, Mark.

Don't take only *my* word for it, though. Lend an ear to Robert B. McGee, Q.C., one of the top criminal lawyers in Toronto. Bob has a story about his friend Sidney R. Roebuck, who retired recently after twenty years of service on the Provincial Court (Criminal Division). McGee and a mob of other guests were convulsed when Judge Roebuck told the tale at his retirement dinner.

"Sid Roebuck does not suffer fools gladly, especially fools who are late for court," McGee notes for the record. "This sort of thing has always raised his dander."

One day, in the late 1980s, Judge Roebuck had an unusually skimpy docket to deal with — an assault case was the only contested matter before the court.

His Honor entered the courtroom, in Etobicoke, in west-end Toronto, precisely at ten that morning. The Crown Attorney was present, and so were his witnesses. The accused was there, too. But his counsel wasn't.

"Where's your lawyer?" the judge asked the prisoner at the bar.

"I don't know, sir." the man replied.

Judge Roebuck, extremely upset, recessed court pending the arrival of defense counsel. He told the court clerk to notify him as soon as the lawyer showed up.

At eleven-thirty, the clerk advised the judge that the lawyer had just arrived.

"By this time, I was fit to be tied," Roebuck later told his dinner audience. "I stormed back into court, slammed my books down on the bench, glared at the young lawyer who stood before me and told him: '*You should have been here at ten o'clock!*'

"After a long pause, the lawyer looked at me and said, 'Why? What happened?'

"I couldn't help myself. I started to laugh, and I couldn't stop. I recessed court again — in a big hurry — so I could go back to my office and settle down."

It's fortunate indeed that laughter erupts from time to time in the courtrooms of the nation. If, perish the thought, it were banished from the halls of justice, the tension level in our courts, usually high to begin with, could become unbearable. In such super-charged surroundings, a good old-fashioned giggle or guffaw can bring instant — and blessed — relief to all concerned. As a veteran lawyer once remarked, "The machinery of justice moves more smoothly when greased with a little humor."

Trial lawyers supply plenty of the aforementioned grease. As warriors in countless legal battles, they've learned that firing off a funny line sometimes fells the foe faster than conventional weapons. A touch of humor can disarm a witness, jolly up a too-tense judge, and swiftly create a more relaxed, productive atmosphere in court. As well as snapping the tension, it also zaps another old enemy — boredom. And, to boot, a little levity goes a long way in helping to persuade. Pianist-comedian Victor Borge put it perfectly: "Laughter is the shortest distance between two people."

Let's drop in on some more lawyers and see what they've done to relieve what's been called "the eternal seriousness" of their profession. I present herewith a bevy of barristers who seek to prove beyond a reasonable doubt that there are moments when the pursuit of justice is a laughing matter.

Sudbury, Ontario, lawyer Richard A. Pharand, Q.C., tells a tale that has a vaudevillian ring to it:

"My partner, Stephen L. McDonald, relates that during a Supreme Court trial in Sudbury his client, the plaintiff, was subjected to a very effective cross-examination. During his cross-examination the plaintiff kept saying that if his daughter-in-law, who'd moved to Vancouver, were present in court she could confirm his evidence.

"Stephen's wife had been in court during the five-day trial, watching her man in action.

"During argument, counsel for the defendant attacked the plaintiff's credibility. Mistaking Stephen's wife for the daughter-in-law, he stated that the daughter-in-law was 'a lady who [had] sat in the courtroom for five days' and had had plenty of opportunity to testify.

"'I fail to understand why this lady didn't come forward and give evidence,' the defendant's lawyer told the judge.

"At that moment, Stephen interrupted his opponent', and said: 'That was no lady — that was my wife.'"

In a case argued in the Supreme Court of Canada several years ago, Vancouver lawyer Sidney B. Simons contended that his client should never have been prosecuted because the Crown, in violation of the Canadian Charter of Rights and Freedoms, took far too long in laying charges and proceeding with them in court.

Simons, who's known affectionately as "Slippery Sid," told me about the case during a long, pleasant conversation I had with him in his law office. In the course of our talk, he reconstructed some of the dialogue that passed between him and one of the judges of Canada's highest court.

Towards the end of his argument, Sid reported, the judge said, "Well, Mr. Simons, what you're complaining of here is that the Vancouver Police Department took fifteen months before they charged this man, and another three months before they arrested him, and then several more months before proceeding in court — something like twenty or twenty-one months, all told."

"Well, yes," Sid replied, "that's part of it, My Lord — if you ignore altogether the loss of some court exhibits, the death of two witnesses and the departure of another witness to California and his unavailability to testify at the trial."

"Oh," said the judge, "the Vancouver police, I'm sure, are very busy. They can't go out and stay with a case and investigate it from start to finish — like Kojak."

There was a pause, and then Sid said, "Kojak, My Lord? Kojak? Oh, yes, My Lord, Kojak — that television personality."

The court was starting to titter by this time, and Sid continued, "Yes, I'm not terribly familiar with Kojak, My Lord, but doesn't he solve every one of his cases in just under an hour?"

The accused was Robin Wood, but the judge, in a recent case in Moncton, New Brunswick, mistakenly called the name "Robin Hood."

When no one answered, Crown Prosecutor Anthony Allman quipped: "Your Honor, the Sheriff of Nottingham is probably out looking for him."

Daphne Zander, a court clerk in Pembroke, Ontario, recalls a case in which a local lawyer was prosecuting a man under the Income Tax Act.

"I'm not trying to make a federal case out of this, Your Honor," the lawyer declared. "Oh, my God, it *is* a federal case!"

Rosemary Rideout of Nova Scotia Legal Aid files this dispatch:

"Lee Mitchell, a staff lawyer with the Legal Aid program in Nova Scotia, was defending a client charged with stealing a musical instrument, a cow bell, from a local music store.

"In summing up his client's defense, Mitchell advised the court that the accused was under a lot of stress 'and perhaps acted inappropriately, as he didn't even have a cow.'"

Back in the 1960s, before drivers who'd imbibed were obliged to submit to a breathalyzer test, Toronto lawyer Garry K. Braund, Q.C., represented a woman charged with impaired driving.

The investigating officer testified that he "detected the smell of an alcoholic beverage" on the breath of the accused, but he conceded that she walked pretty steadily, her eyes weren't glassy, and she didn't slur her words when speaking. However, he said, her car crossed slightly over the center line of the road several times.

Evidence also disclosed that the accused had been driving in her stocking feet — which, said Braund, explained the erratic driving.

"A lot of women do that sort of thing, but I've never heard of a man doing it," the judge observed. "I wonder why so many women drive with their shoes off."

"Your Honor," said Braund, tongue in cheek and on his way to a win, "perhaps women care more than men about saving their soles."

In days of yore, a lawyer could hardly function in court unless he knew — and could speak — nearly as much Latin as a cardinal. As the centuries rolled by, however, it became increasingly less important to be steeped in the lingo of the ancient Romans. But even in today's legal world there's a fair bit of life left in this so-called dead language.

Certain Latin expressions are still flung around with great gusto in our courts of justice, and it behooves a barrister to have more than a nodding acquaintance with them. If he or she is deficient in this department, why, he or she might unwittingly cause an outbreak of learned laughter. Take *sui juris*, for example, and, while you're at it, why not ponder the ever-popular *functus officio*?

Sui juris means "of full legal capacity." If you're s*ui juris,* you can validly enter into contracts and bind yourself by legal obligation, uncontrolled by any other person.

Mr. Justice George L. Murray of the Supreme Court of British Columbia recalls a Vancouver lawyer who ran afoul of this hallowed phrase.

One day, in the 1950s, the lawyer appeared before Mr. Justice Alexander Manson and asked him to approve the appointment of a particular person as "administrator without bond" in an estate. The deceased's children had signed documents in which they consented to the appointment, and the documents were filed in court.

Mr. Justice Manson, one of the crankiest and most dreaded jurists in the history of the province, was known far and wide as "the Hanging Judge." Lawyers avoided him whenever possible, and if there was no escaping him they gritted their teeth and hoped for the best. That's the way it was on the day in question.

"Are all the children *sui juris?*" growled His Lordship.

"Oh, yes, My Lord," said the lawyer, whose mind had gone blank. "They're all very healthy."

That old rascal *functus officio* means "having discharged his duty." For example, if a judge has heard a case and rendered judgment he can't cancel his decision and retry the case. He's *functus*, as lawyers and judges say for short.

Ottawa lawyer John ("Jake") Dunlap, Q.C., one of Canada's foremost wits, recalls a case in which that pesky little word popped up. Jake brought a motion asking for a certain order and his opponent, a hotshot Toronto counsel, put up vigorous opposition.

"That can't be done," he declared. "His Honor is *functus.*"

"Your Honor," said Jake, "in the Ottawa Valley, where I come from, we pronounce that word just a bit differently."

If the perfect Latin phrase eludes you, why not invent one? In 1988, Associate Chief Justice Tevie H. Miller, of the Court of Queen's Bench of Alberta, encountered a case in point:

"Although there are too few opportunities in open court for lawyers to make effective use of witty repartee, I was delighted to preside over the following example.

"Two lawyers approached me and asked if I could hear an urgent matter of interim custody of a young child, as the parents were separated and unable to reach any agreement. I agreed to hear the application but advised the lawyers that I had already scheduled another application to be heard from 2:00 P.M. to 3:00 P.M. and had agreed to preside over a Bar Admission ceremony at 4:00 P.M.

"I was assured that the interim custody application could be heard in the one hour available. As it happened, the first application ran overtime but counsel were still confident they could complete their matter before 4:00 P.M.

"The first lawyer took far longer than estimated and the second lawyer was in full flight in the middle of her argument when I noticed it was almost 4:00 P.M. and people were arriving in the courtroom to attend the Bar Admission ceremony.

"I interrupted the lawyer in mid-sentence to say that I would adjourn forthwith to get ready for the ceremony but would reconvene to hear the rest of her argument right after the conclusion of the admission. She looked a little startled at my interruption.

"Half an hour later, I recommenced the custody hearing and called upon the lawyer to continue with her argument. She started off by saying that she had never been cut off in mid-sentence by a judge before and felt she was 'suffering from *custodius interruptus.*'

"Nevertheless, she recovered quickly from this phenomenon and continued to press her client's case with considerable success."

My favorite story about Latin in the courtroom is a classic — and true — tale that hales from Ireland. It has to do with an ancient legal maxim, a judicial jawbreaker that reads as follows: *Cujus est solum ejus est usque ad coelum et ad inferos.* Translated literally, that says: "Whose is the soil, his it is, even to heaven and to the middle of the earth." Or to put it another way: "If you own land, you own all the way up and all the way down."

A century ago, while arguing a case involving the invasion of aerial rights over land, a well-known Irish counsel was interrupted by the judge, who said: "That's all very well and good, Mr. Sullivan, but have your clients never heard of the maxim, *Cujus est solum ejus est usque ad coelum et ad inferos?*"

"My Lord," the lawyer replied, "the peasants of Northern Ireland talk of little else!"

Swamped with work, and against the wishes of the local bar, a Dublin judge announced that he was going to hold court on Good Friday. "The better the day, the better the deed," he declared.

"If you do, My Lord," said one of the complaining counsel, "you'll be the first judge to sit on Good Friday since Pontius Pilate."

In a Toronto courtroom, in 1986, a lawyer made a suggestion that, fortunately for zillions of people, still hasn't been implemented. Provincial Court Judge Sydney M. Harris, who presided at the trial of a man charged with sexual assault, preserved this dialogue for posterity:

Q. I take it you would reject the suggestion that you had entered into an agreement that night with Mr. Brock, when he was in your room, to have sexual intercourse with him for a payment, or in exchange for a payment by him to you, of fifty dollars for that act of intercourse?

A. Would you repeat that, please?

JUDGE: Would you put it in the kind of wording the witness will understand, instead of the elaborate wording you just devised?

LAWYER: I'll simplify it, Your Honor.

JUDGE: What he's asking you is, did you agree to have intercourse for fifty dollars?

A. No.

JUDGE: That was the question, wasn't it?

LAWYER: Yes. A lawyer should be paid by the word.

Some lawyers talk far too fast in court. Bernard Loomis, a court reporter in Vernon, British Columbia, could barely keep up with a barrister who went full throttle while questioning his client, a very large woman who was the petitioner in a divorce action. Thanks to Bernard, we have this specimen of unbridled speed:

Q. And you are a house and your husband is —

JUDGE: What did you call her?

LAWYER I'm sorry, My Lord?

JUDGE: Did I hear you call her a house?

LAWYER: I'm sorry, My Lord. Sometimes my mouth gets ahead of my brains. I meant a housewife.

Pelly Crossing ain't exactly a metropolis. It's a tiny settlement, located about two hundred miles north of Whitehorse in the Yukon Territory, and at last count only 177 folks called it home.

"There's little or nothing to do there," court reporter Sharon Gately reports, "and it's the place that the court staff least likes to go to."

Sharon sent me a short transcript that certainly confirms her assessment.

"A trial was being held in Whitehorse before Territorial Court Judge Dwayne Rowe, and a member of the Royal Canadian Mounted Police was testifying," Sharon says by way of introduction. "Whitehorse lawyer P. S. O'Brien was just concluding his cross-examination of the Mountie and the Crown Attorney, D. R. Beardall, also of Whitehorse, was ready to call the next witness."

Now, let's take a squint at the transcript:

MR. O'BRIEN: Thank you, Corporal. Those are my questions.

MR. BEARDALL: No re-examination.

JUDGE ROWE: Thank you very much. You're free to go straight back to Pelly now.

CORPORAL: Oh, joy, Your Honor!

MR. BEARDALL: You shouldn't be sentencing the *witnesses*, Your Honor!

The aforementioned Judge Dwayne Rowe, who at this writing is a mere tad of forty-eight, is an extremely versatile and funny fellow. Before joining the Territorial Court of the Yukon, he was an outstanding criminal lawyer in Peace River, Edmonton, and Calgary, and he served for a spell on the Provincial Court (Criminal Division) of Alberta. At various times he's also been a newspaperman, radio personality, television comedy writer, stand-up comic, and prolific composer of "one-liners" for Joan Rivers and other big-name entertainers. Indeed, some of his exploits and antics were chronicled in my book, *More Court Jesters*.

Since 1988, Rowe's been hearing and deciding highly technical revenue cases all over the country, as a Deputy Judge of the Tax Court of Canada. He has a yarn from that court that will be of particular interest to football fans.

"A judge of the Tax Court, sitting in Calgary, had to decide whether a particular lodge in the nearby Kananaskis area of Alberta was or was not a business," Judge Rowe told me, "and that depended on whether or not it had 'a reasonable expectation of making a profit.'

"Several years ago, the owner of the lodge got into financial difficulties. The lodge went into receivership and some time later a bank, which had been appointed Receiver, sold the lodge to Joe Barnes, the quarterback of the Calgary Stampeders.

"One of the lawyers who appeared before the court, sorting out who was who and who did what, said, 'Now, have I got this right, Joe Barnes was the quarterback and the bank was the Receiver?'"

A judge can "stay" — in effect, put on hold — any legal proceeding that appears to be frivolous or taken for the purpose of delay, or which he considers to be "an abuse of the process of the court."

Provincial Court Judge Derek T. Hogg of Toronto recalls a case in which one of his fellow jurists and a rookie lawyer obviously weren't on the same wavelength.

One morning, on towards noon, it seemed to the judge that the lawyer was suggesting, or getting ready to suggest, that the case should be put in limbo because the Crown was playing dirty pool. So the judge, trying to help out a bit, asked the lawyer, "Are you making a motion to stay?"

"Oh, no, Your Honor," counsel replied, "I have a luncheon date today."

The best defense is an offense, they say. Chief Justice Allan McEachern, of the Supreme Court of British Columbia, tells of a case in point:

"Henry Castillou, later a County Court Judge and the loudest voice in British Columbia, was late for an afternoon sitting of the Court of Appeal. His absence was not noted until the court was on the bench. He burst into the courtroom like a ship in full sail and, with the wit of good counsel, quickly assessed the situation and exclaimed: 'Oh, I'm sorry, Milords, I thought we'd adjourned until 2:34 P.M.'"

A lawyer should pick his words ever so carefully in courts, right? And he should never say anything that might offend the judge, right? Then the Golden Goof Award should go to the lawyer who, in 1989, told a jury: "The reason we selected the twelve of you to hear this matter is because we wanted people to hear it who had common sense. Otherwise, we'd just have the judge hear the case."

Courtroom etiquette also dictates that, no matter what the provocation, counsel must refrain from making personal cracks about the judge. Lawyers sometimes have trouble with this commandment.

Back in the 1950s, for example, a lawyer was asked to represent a twelve-year-old boy who was charged with fondling himself in public.

The judge listened carefully to the evidence, as well as counsel's submissions, and then gave some fatherly advice: "This sort of thing will get you nowhere, Tommy, and if you don't believe me, just ask your lawyer."

"I shall defer to Your Honor's greater experience," the lawyer replied.

One day, in the 1940s, magistrate William K. ("Willie") MacGregor was presiding in Killaloe, in the Ottawa Valley, when a sharply dressed Toronto lawyer plunked down a stack of law books and entered a not-guilty plea on behalf of a young fellow charged with assault.

After all the evidence had been presented, the lawyer launched a learned argument, the likes of which MacGregor had never heard. A few minutes later, when he'd had enough, His Worship leaned forward and delivered a message that brought him instant — and eternal — fame throughout the Valley and beyond.

"That might be the law where you come from," he told the startled young lawyer, "but it ain't the law in Killaloe!"

Over the years, the village of Killaloe (population 700 and change) has been the scene of many a rowdy altercation, in and out of court, and it's spawned some pretty unorthodox local "laws," one of which reads as follows: "In Killaloe, it ain't assault unless the other guy goes to the hospital."

Killaloe is more subdued today, but back in the 1940s and '50s, when Renfrew lawyer Jim Maloney was undisputed champion of all Valley courtrooms, anything might happen — and often did.

"Maloney was a super trial lawyer," says William T. Green, Q.C., of Ottawa. "Not just in the Valley, but in Ottawa and Toronto and anywhere else he took on a case."

Green recently reminisced about a case Jim Maloney defended in those free-wheeling days in — you guessed it — Killaloe.

The accused was charged with having an open bottle of liquor in his car. The bottle, with several ounces of colorless fluid in it, had been put into evidence and a tag, marked "Exhibit 1," dangled from its neck.

"Give me that exhibit," Maloney said to the court clerk, as the arresting officer stood in the witness box, waiting to be cross-examined.

Maloney tore the tag off the bottle and, approaching the witness, he said, "Constable, you said the bottle contains gin?"

"Yes, sir."

"Did you have it analyzed at a laboratory?"

"No, I didn't."

"Well, would you agree that it looks like water?"

"Yes, sir."

"Did you *taste* it?"

"No, I didn't."

"Did you *smell* it?"

"No."

Maloney removed the cap from the bottle and sniffed.

"It smells like water to me," he said, and then he tilted his head back and quaffed the contents.

"Your Worship," he announced, "it's water."

The accused was acquitted.

A few years ago, another Ottawa lawyer, John R. Wrigley, wrote to me about Jim Maloney's brother, Arthur, who practiced in Toronto and was widely recognized as one of the best courtroom lawyers in Canada. Like Jim, Arthur was practically fearless. He *had* to have plenty of nerve to stand up to cranky judges as often as he did. In his letter, John Wrigley recalled one such occasion:

"Arthur was defending a man charged with several counts of indecent assault. The accused was trained in acupuncture and his method of diagnosis was to insert needles into the arms of unsuspecting women. If the points of entry became inflamed, this was taken as evidence of a general infection which would require — you got it! — a further examination of the patient's personal parts.

"The defense called an expert witness to testify as to the validity of such a procedure and Mr. Maloney and the trial judge had repeated disagreements on its admissibility as evidence.

"At the conclusion of his questioning, Mr. Maloney slowly turned his gaze toward the trial judge and asked one last question of his witness: 'Tell me, sir, would acupuncture be of assistance in treating an elderly gentleman with a vile temper?'"

An American lawyer was much more diplomatic than Art Maloney when he hit rough weather in the Supreme Court of the United States. Midway through his argument, he stated a proposition of law and declared that there could be little, if any, doubt as to its correctness.

"Why, I've never heard of such a thing!" growled one of the Justices. "You don't mean to tell us that that's the law, do you?"

The lawyer bowed from the hips and replied, "It was, before Your Honor spoke."

All things considered, clients cause lawyers more grief in court than judges do — especially gabby clients who don't know when to shut up.

Denis Archambault, a lawyer in Prince George, British Columbia, recalls the troublesome time a colleague of his had trying to muzzle a woman client who kept tugging at his sleeve and talking to him, and the judge, during her trial.

Several times, the lawyer told her to cease and desist. At first, he was even nice about it, explaining quietly that when she interrupted him she ruined his train of thought, irritated the judge and the other lawyer, and delayed the trial as well.

"Look," he told her during a recess, "you could lose the case because of this sort of thing. Just let me do the talking. I know what I'm doing."

But the interruptions continued — tug, tug, yap, yap — and the exasperated lawyer turned on his client and, in so doing, brought the house down.

"Madam," he fairly shouted, "do you have a dog at home?"

"Well, yes."

"Do you do the barking?"

Of course, a lawyer's opponent can cause plenty of trouble, too. Provincial Court Judge James A. Fontana of Ottawa particularly recalls one "learned friend" who gave him a devil of a time in court. All right, Your Honor, let's have the grisly details:

"In 1966, as a neophyte prosecutor in Ottawa, I had been warned about the formidable defense counsel, W. Dan Chilcott, who is now Mr. Justice Chilcott of the Supreme Court of Ontario. 'Be prepared,' I was told in no uncertain terms by my boss, John Cassells, now Judge Cassells of the Provincial Court (Criminal Division).

"The dreaded day finally arrived when I came nose to nose with Dan on a trial, his client having been charged with several break-and-enters in and around a small community outside Ottawa.

"I had been up all night preparing the case, and I was ready. Nothing had been overlooked. I paraded my witnesses.

"The general-store owner testified about a break-in. Chilcott cross-examined, asking, finally, whether a post-hole auger had been stolen. None had. Did the owner have any post-hole augers on the premises at the time? He didn't.

"I called the owner of the service station who was likewise cross-examined by Chilcott. Again, at the end, the questions about post-hole augers. No, none had been taken. No, there had been none on the premises.

"I called a homeowner who had been broken into. At the end of his cross-examination, the same thing about post-hole augers.

"By this time I was frantic. What trick was Chilcott up to? What was all this about post-hole augers? What had I missed in preparation? Finally, in desperation, I turned to the investigating officer who was assisting me and asked him to check the file. No answer was to be found there.

"At last, the case was completed. The defence called no evidence and the accused was found guilty on some of the charges, not guilty on others.

"I couldn't stand it any longer and went over to Dan, who was busy gathering up his papers.

"'Mr. Chilcott,' I asked, 'what's all this business about post-hole augers? Was it a red herring to throw me off stride?'

"'Not really,' he replied. 'You see, I have a cottage up near where all those witnesses live, and I want to put in a new fence, but I can't find a post-hole auger to rent anywhere. Say, you don't know where I can get one, do you?'"

Former Senator Richard A. Donahoe, Q.C., had a long association with my father, Vincent C. MacDonald, who was Dean of Law at Dalhousie University in the late 1930s and '40s and later sat on the Supreme Court of Nova Scotia. Dick, as everyone called him, studied under my father, and over the years he argued many cases before him. He distinguished himself as a lawyer, as mayor of Halifax, and as a Progressive Conservative member of the provincial legislature. For several years prior to his appointment to the Canadian Senate, he was attorney-general of Nova Scotia.

Dick knew that for many years before going on the bench Dad had been an active member of the Liberal Party, and had even served for a while as private secretary to Prime Minister William Lyon Mackenzie King. He also knew that my father had a great sense of humor and that if he told me a particular story he'd been wanting to tell me (a) it wouldn't make my old man revolve in his grave and (b) if perchance it did, it would surely be from laughter.

So, one day in 1987, Senator Donahoe grabbed a leaky ball-point pen and scribbled these words, which I bequeath to anyone who'd like to have them:

"In the years when I was attorney-general and your father was on the Supreme Court, during an election, I went to Sutherland's River to speak in support of a colleague. We spoke in a high-school auditorium and, before going in, left our coats and hats in a classroom.

"After the meeting, when we went for our coats we found that some joker had written this verse on the blackboard:

> Vote Tory,
> Live in glory.
> Vote Grit,
> Live in shit.

"I hurried to clean the board, but never forgot the sentiments.

"Some time later, I met your father in the courthouse, near the Judge's Entrance. He said, 'You're just the man I want to see. Come with me.'

"He led me outside to the curb and said, 'Turn around.'

"I did, and faced the courthouse, which was disfigured with pigeon droppings from top to bottom.

"'Isn't that disgraceful?' your father said. 'What are you going to do about it?'

"I said, 'That's the responsibility of the Courthouse Commission, not mine, but let me tell you a story.'

"I told him of the words written on the blackboard and then I said, 'My Lord, with your political record, you can't expect anything better.'"

Provincial Court Judge C. Emerson Perkins, of Chatham, Ontario, has sent me a gaggle of good stories. Here, in two sentences, is one of his latest:

"Advertising slogans can create humor in the solemnity of court.

"As one o'clock approached, Judge 'Red' Hendriksen remembered that he had an important appointment for lunch, and as H. J. O'Brien, Q.C., droned on, speaking to sentence for his client, he noticed that Judge Hendriksen was wringing his hands, and he said, 'Your Honor, is anything wrong?' to which the judge replied, 'It's after one o'clock and I'm about to have a Big Mac attack,' after which Mr. O'Brien struck a telling blow for his client by saying, 'Please don't forget that my client also deserves a break today.'"

4

THAT WAS A GOOD ONE, YOUR HONOR

AND IF I LAUGH AT ANY MORTAL THING,

'TIS THAT I MAY NOT WEEP.

Lord Byron

HE WHO LAUGHS, LASTS.

Mary Pettibone Poole

There are a great many jobs easier than sitting in judgment on one's fellow human beings. Scaling mountain peaks is one that springs to mind.

"Night Court" fans mightn't believe this, but judging is a lonely, deadly serious, pressure-packed occupation. With the territory come heaps of homework, plenty of agonizing over judgments, loads of awesome responsibility, and a steady succession of sorrowful, often boring cases to be decided by the mere mortal who's up there on the bench.

You don't have to be a shrink to know that if that state of affairs continued unabated a judge could easily flip his or her wig. Unless, of course, laughter rides to the rescue — as, mercifully, it often does.

There's nothing like a giggle or a guffaw to break the tension and rejuvenate a judge for another round or two. Indeed, some jocular jurists, in desperate need of a humor break, have the happy knack of generating levity almost at will. The instant relief that results therefrom enables them to stay in possession of their marbles at all times and, I'm sure, keeps them young at heart well into their old age.

I've checked out a mob of such fortunate folks, preserving sundry remarks they've made in court with laughter aforethought. Let's examine some of the evidence:

Provincial Court Judge James D. Reardon, of Yarmouth, Nova Scotia, tells of a case heard down his way.

A few years ago, a couple of fellows were charged with "hooping" lobsters out of season. The "hoop" that's used in the commission of this dastardly — and pretty common — offense is about two feet in diameter, and it has a canvas base with a slit on the top. Through this slit the culprits drop dead herring (or, if they're hard of herring, anything else that will lead lobsters astray).

When the hoop is submerged in shallow water near shore, lobsters fall on top of it and drop to the bottom of the contraption. One man, standing in the water, retrieves the hoop and tosses it to his accomplice on the shore. He dumps the lobsters into a bag and then the simple process is repeated, as often as desired.

In court, the prosecutor led evidence to show that the accused men followed the procedure described above.

But something crucial was missing.

"Do you have the hoop in court today to present as an exhibit in this trial?" asked Judge John Nichols.

"No, I'm sorry, Your Honor, I don't," the prosecutor replied.

"I'm dismissing the charges," said Judge Nichols, "for you have a hoopless case."

Judge Ray Stortini, of Sault Ste. Marie, Ontario, has sent me many humorous stories. Here, in his own words, is one of his latest:

"I recently had a difficult child-abuse problem to resolve. My confrère had ordered supervised access in the town of Wawa. The parents could not agree on a suitable supervisor. I asked counsel if they could suggest a suitable person. Negative. I then asked if the child attended church and was told that she attended St. Monica's Church in Wawa.

"I suggested, and it was agreed, that the parish priest, Father Randy, be the supervisor. I ventured that Father Randy might be able to bring the family to a point of less bitterness and hostility. I said he could act as a catalyst — a Roman Catalyst."

Calgary court reporter Rosemary MacDonald has a story about the late Judge Ray Thomas of the Provincial Court in Edmonton:

"A man came before Judge Thomas and pleaded guilty to leaving a stop sign when it was unsafe to do so. The specified penalty was a fine of twenty-five dollars, but before imposing sentence, His Honor asked the accused if he had anything to say.

"The man explained that he was driving with his mother-in-law, had come to a full stop at the sign, but had so much stuff in the car he couldn't see if it was clear. His mother-in-law told him it was, but when he pulled out he was struck from the right side.

"Judge Thomas, having listened sympathetically, said: 'That'll be twenty-five dollars — ten dollars for leaving the stop sign when it was unsafe, and fifteen dollars for listening to your mother-in-law.'"

In a Winnipeg courtroom in 1988, Mr. Justice John Scollin put the ham in Hamlet.

During a criminal trial in the Manitoba Court of Queen's Bench, the Crown Attorney sheepishly confessed that he'd accidentally submitted a bit of evidence from another case:

"It has been brought to my attention that Exhibit 2B is, in fact, from an unrelated case and should be withdrawn."

Upon hearing this, His Lordship, in his Scottish brogue, dramatically chortled: "Is it 2B or not 2B? That is the question!"

Don Lindal of Winnipeg sends another story about the irrepressible Mr. Justice Scollin:

Traditionally, when a judge enters a courtroom, the court clerk, facing the lawyers and spectators, solemnly intones: "Order! All rise!"

But one day, in 1987, a rookie clerk forgot herself. When His

Lordship appeared, she turned to him and chirped with innocent brightness:

"Hello!"

This drew chuckles from everyone within earshot, and when it was time for lunch, Mr. Justice Scollin rose and declared:

"We are adjourned until two o'clock."

Then, glancing at the clerk, he wondered out loud:

"Or should I just say goodbye?"

A judge of the Supreme Court of Ontario didn't fare as well when he announced a recess. Toronto court reporter Shirley Hooper was on hand, capturing the hungry jurist's every word. According to the transcript, this is what he said to one of the lawyers:

HIS LORDSHIP: Perhaps this might be a good point to adjourn for lunch.

COUNSEL: Certainly, My Lord.

HIS LORDSHIP: We will return at two-fifteen to two-thirty. Two-fifteen. If I am here, we will start. If I am not here till two-thirty, we won't start, but I will try to be here, and I want the rest of your people to be here at two-fifteen, if you can, but if you can't, I won't criticize you because I may not be here, so be here at two-fifteen, if you can, please.

My thanks to Toronto lawyer Stanley G. Fisher, Q.C., for sending me a copy of an Alberta court decision that should be required reading in every law school in the land. It has to do with the important but deadly dull subject of construction liens, and legions of lawyers are delighted that in this landmark ruling the stodgy old doctrine of *stare decisis* gets the kind of clarification it has sorely needed for many centuries.

For those who haven't made its acquaintance, *stare decisis* is Latin shorthand for the "sacred principle" of law which states that decisions of higher courts must be followed by lower courts.

The hero of this story is M. B. Funduk of Edmonton, a man who holds the judge-like position of "Master in Chambers" of the Court of Queen's Bench of Alberta. These are the words that brought him instant fame:

"Any legal system which has a judicial appeals process inherently creates a pecking order for the judiciary regarding where judicial decisions stand on the legal ladder.

"I am bound by decisions of the Queen's Bench judges, by decisions of the Alberta Court of Appeal, and by decisions of the Supreme Court of Canada. Very simply, Masters in Chambers of a superior trial court occupy the bottom rung of the superior courts' judicial ladder.

"I do not over-rule decisions of a judge of this court. The judicial pecking order does not permit little peckers to over-rule big peckers. It is the other way around."

Which reminds me . . .

For quite some time, until recently, the Ontario Pork Producers Marketing Board had a catchy slogan that read, "Put Pork On Your Fork."

One autumn day in 1985, a man entered a Toronto supermarket and, according to a report filed in court, was seen to stash "two large packages of spareribs" — $11.45 worth — "down the front of his pants." He was nabbed outside the store and charged with theft under $200.

The accused pleaded guilty before Provincial Court Judge J. S. Climans, who, in passing sentence, noted for the record:

"I guess he's been taking the advertising very seriously. You know, it's supposed to be 'Pork On Your Fork' — not 'Pork On Your Dork.'"

And that reminds me of still another yarn, told to me by Waterloo, Ontario, lawyer Rudy Kominek:

In Sarnia, Ontario, back in the 1940s, a Quebec man pleaded not guilty to a charge of indecent exposure. The evidence disclosed that the accused had had too much to drink one Saturday night and was seen relieving himself behind a tree. The court was also told that the man was married and had fourteen children.

The magistrate, wishing to give the visitor a break, ruled as follows: "I don't think this man is guilty of indecent exposure. He just hasn't had time to do up his fly."

Provincial Court Judge Garrett A. Handrigan, of Grand Bank, Newfoundland, tells of a youth who appeared in court to face a charge of careless driving. His TransAm had registered 140 kilometers per hour on a radar screen, and in the police chase that followed, said TransAm scored even higher — 160 to 170 km/h — before yielding to a roadblock. Despite all of this, the prosecutor didn't ask for a licence suspension.

The accused, who was anxious to get things over with, pleaded guilty to the charge.

"I've got to get a job, but I haven't been able to get one here in Newfoundland," he told the judge. "I'm going to try Toronto. In fact, I'm flying there tomorrow."

"By Air Canada or TransAm?" His Honor inquired.

In another Newfoundland case, a St. John's magistrate was disappointed that a certain young woman was back in court, facing her umpteenth prostitution charge.

"The last time you were here, Geraldine, you indicated you were going to give up this sordid way of life," His Worship reminded the accused.

"I know."

"But you haven't."

"That's right."

"Have you been thinking about it?"

"Not much."

"Why not do what you said you were going to do?"

"Nah."

"You'll feel so much better about yourself if you just take the bull by the horns and give up prostitution forever."

"I don't want to."

"Well, would you give it up for *Lent*?"

Edmonton lawyer Peggy Blair tells of a recent case in the Alberta Court of Appeal. A prostitute appealed her jail sentence, stating that she should only have been fined or given a term of probation. Mr. Justice John McClung asked her counsel: "Are you submitting that a proposition should never be followed by a sentence?"

The Honorable Allan McEachern, Chief Justice of the Supreme Court of British Columbia, reminisces: "In a case before Mr. Justice Harry Sullivan and a jury Mr. T. O. Griffiths was having the plaintiff's doctor describe the treatment the plaintiff had received. The plaintiff himself had previously described the horrible agonies of prolonged traction.

"When the doctor said that he prescribed traction, Mr. Justice Sullivan stopped him and asked, 'Oh, tell us, doctor — what is traction?'

"After the explanation was given, Mr. Justice Sullivan said, looking right at the jury with a wide smile on his face. 'Oh, you mean you tie these ropes to the plaintiff's foot so you can pull his leg, just as he's been pulling ours for the last two days?'"

Toronto lawyer Eric K. Grossman also has a yarn about a personal injury action — one that arose out of a rear-end motor-vehicle collision.

"At trial, counsel were called into the judge's chambers to speak about the use of subpoenas to obtain hospital records pertaining to the pre-accident health of the plaintiff," Eric writes. "The plaintiff's lawyer, William Morris, Q.C., of Hamilton, contended that his client's medical condition prior to the accident was irrelevant — especially records pertaining to his hospitilization for hemorrhoid surgery some twelve years earlier.

"To this, the judge, Mr. Justice John Holland, replied: 'Mr. Morris, surely you're not arguing that the hemorrhoid records are not relevant. After all, this is a case about a *rear-end* collision!'"

Provincial Court Judge James A. Fontana of Ottawa tells a tale about a former member of that court, Judge Bruce Hunter, of Winchester, Ontario.

He reports that whenever Judge Hunter had a case involving a search warrant, he always insisted that the warrant itself be filed as an exhibit.

One day, Judge Hunter was hearing such a case in a small town. The town constable testified that he had carried out the search warrant. He was about to continue his testimony when Judge Hunter interrupted to tell him to produce the warrant and enter it as an exhibit. Alas, the hapless constable didn't have it with him.

"Where is it, constable?" asked the judge.

"I don't know, Your Honor."

"Well, go look for it."

"Now?"

"Now."

The constable stepped out of the witness box, left the court-room, and ran down to the police station, which was only about half a block away. Judge Hunter didn't adjourn court. The constable returned five minutes later, sweating and out of breath.

"You found the warrant?" Judge Hunter inquired.

"I did, Your Honor."

"File it, then."

The warrant was made Exhibit 1 and the case continued with the constable describing how he went to the address to carry out the warrant and the lady of the house got hostile and abusive with him.

"When I presented the warrant, she said something to me I can't repeat in court, Your Honor."

"Tell me. The court's heard it all before."

"I can't, Your Honor."

"*Tell* me! It's a *court order*!"

"Well, Your Honor, she told me to shove the warrant up my arse!"

"So that explains it," said the judge. "*That's* where the warrant's been all this time!"

Vancouver lawyer Robert H. Guile, Q.C., has written and privately distributed an excellent book on his uncle, John Oswald Wilson, who served for many years as a County Court judge in the interior of British Columbia and then was promoted to the Supreme Court of British Columbia and, after that, to the Court of Appeal of the province. "J.O.W.," as his friends all called him, was born and raised in the British Columbia interior and practiced law there for a couple of decades before he went on the bench.

Shortly after his appointment to the Supreme Court of British Columbia, the new judge, who would one day become Chief Justice of that court, was sent to hear cases in Pouce Coupé, away up the line near Dawson Creek.

"At that time there was nothing in Pouce Coupé except the bar, the hotel, the beer parlor and the courthouse," writes Bob Guile. "They had fortunately just completed a second floor to the hotel, on which there were several rooms. There was no plumbing at that time, except that on the second floor they had taken one of those rooms and converted it into a bathroom. As a necessary background, one should know that J.O.W. was well known up in that area from the activities of his youth, so that practically everyone up there knew him.

"When my uncle went there to preside at the assizes, they were installing this bathroom and the work had not been completed. J.O.W. had run into some people who'd insisted he have a drink and by the time he went to his room he was very anxious to attend upon the bathroom facilities.

"He ran down the hall, tearing off his garments as he went, got to the bathroom and sat upon the commode in order to perform his functions. At that time the windows had not been put in and there was a man standing at the window painting the window sills.

"The window-painter looked in the window and said, 'Hi, Jack, long time no see.'

"J.O.W. replied, 'Well, this is my first sitting up here.'"

Bob Guile's book has many good quotes from his uncle, including this one:

"I remember a lay magistrate in Quesnel who went to an assize once and heard a Supreme Court judge pronounce the death sentence. When he got back to his own court, he adopted part of his new learning. Finding a man guilty, he said solemnly: 'I hereby order you to pay a fine of five dollars — and may the Lord have mercy on your soul!'"

Mr. Justice Rodman E. Logan, of the Court of Queen's Bench of

New Brunswick, is a second-generation jurist. His father, G. Earle Logan, Q.C., who served for thirty-six years as a stipendiary magistrate, tried thousands of cases in a tiny courtroom over a fire hall in Lancaster, New Brunswick.

One day, a young lawyer we'll call Jones put on a memorable show.

"Jones was being a little melodramatic," Mr. Justice Logan recalls. "He kept backing up as he questioned a witness — back, back, back, until, finally, he stepped through the door. Whereupon my father leaned forward and said, 'Mr. Jones, you're leaving, are you?'"

As you've probably noticed, history has a habit of repeating itself. Now we step forward in time for another backing-up story:

Provincial Court Judge Joe Kennedy, who normally dispenses justice in Bridgewater, Nova Scotia, recently "pinch hit" for a judge in another community, where he presided at the trial of a man charged with assaulting a patron in a pub. Appearing for the Crown was a lawyer, much given to theatrics, who loves to demonstrate things physically in court.

After the Crown had presented a pretty damning case, the defense called its first witness, a huge bloke who was a bouncer at the saloon in question. He gave very strong evidence to the effect that the accused had acted in self-defense. The case for the prosecution hinged on just how well this witness had seen the altercation.

When Crown Counsel asked the bouncer how far away from the fight he'd been, the fellow replied that he wasn't much good at estimating distances.

The prosecutor then walked up to the witness box and told the occupant that he would start to back away.

"Tell me to stop when I'm as far away as you were from the altercation," he said.

"Okay."

The prosecutor started walking backwards.

"Is this far enough?" he asked when he'd reached the railing.

"No."

The prosecutor continued to back up, and when he was

halfway down the aisle in the body of the courtroom he asked loudly, "Now?"

"Not yet! Keep going!"

The prosecutor back-pedaled all the way to the courtroom door, then shouted, "Am I far enough away yet?"

"No — not yet!" the witness hollered back.

And then Judge Kennedy piped up: "Don't forget to send a postcard when you get to Moncton!"

There's no business like show business. . . .

With no apologies to Abbott and Costello, Provincial Court Judge C. Emerson Perkins, of Chatham, Ontario, provides proof positive that humor can rear its lovely head at any time in judicial proceedings — even in a murder case.

I had to sit on this story for a spell because there was a publication ban until trial. But the case is over now (the accused was convicted) and Judge Perkins discloses what happened at the preliminary hearing in January 1989:

"The matter concerned a murder by a Laotian at a Laotian soccer tournament," His Honor writes. "All of the witnesses were Laotians with long unpronounceable names. To our benefit, each had a short name or nickname, such as 'Ta,' 'La,' 'Phon,' 'Dan,' 'Khan,' etc. The accused was 'Tui' and the victim was 'Me.'

"A witness, well into the hearing, was describing the events when he said, 'And then he shot Me.'

"The Crown Attorney, who must have lost concentration for a moment, said, 'Oh, you were shot?'

"The witness replied, 'Oh, no. He shot Me.'

"At this point, I said to defense counsel, 'I hope he doesn't ask, Who's on first?'"

Dr. D. E. L. King, head of the Regional Forensic Pathology Unit at Hamilton Civic Hospitals, checks in with an anecdote about Mr. Justice Peter Cory, an extremely able and patient jurist who served on the trial division of the Supreme Court of Ontario, then on the Ontario Court of Appeal, and now graces the Supreme Court of Canada. The tale arises out of the four-and-a-half-week trial of a charge of attempted murder, in which the jury found the accused guilty of the less serious offense of wounding. Take it away, Doc:

"As a 'professional' medical witness for many years, I have seen and heard a good deal of the lighter side of court work. I think the best, however, occurred during a trial that took place in Ottawa in 1981. I suppose you could call it a case of 'Judicial Act of Contrition.'

"A thirty-year-old man took it into his head to assassinate Prime Minister Trudeau. He brought a sharp knife to do the job but found that the prime minister was too well protected, so he decided to attack instead a senior Army officer in the parking lot at the National Defense Headquarters.

"The officer, with lightning reflexes, deflected the knife, which was aimed at his abdomen or chest. The knife went through his forearm and superficially injured the abdomen, and he survived. The accused was charged with attempted murder. Although he could have been insane at the time, he was found competent to stand trial and, after dismissing a series of defense counsel, he elected to conduct his own defense, which he did surprisingly well.

"The only problem was that his questions to the witnesses usually consisted of a ten-to-fifteen-minute political statement with the question at the end. I am sure that the trial judge, Mr. Justice Peter Cory, must have been hand-picked for this very difficult trial, which went on much longer than expected.

"I was called as an expert witness to give evidence about the actual wounding — whether the attack was such that intent to kill was present, and so on. I spent a very trying afternoon fielding questions, including questions on physics that were just about beyond me.

"Finally I was dismissed, only to be called back the next afternoon because the accused had 'two or three' more questions to put to me. Again the court had to put up with the interminable statement/questions when, suddenly, in the middle of a question, the accused stopped. He must have noticed some slight change in the expression on the judge's face.

"'Am I annoying you, My Lord?' he asked.

"'No,' replied His Lordship, slowly and quietly, 'you're not annoying me.'

"Then, after a short pause, the judge added: 'I tell a lie — but I'm going to confession next week.'"

Mr. Justice Allan Wachowich, of the Court of Queen's Bench of Alberta, is known far and wide for his sense of humor. He's a great kidder, and so is his wife, Bette. His Lordship has a dramatic tale to tell:

"I presided at a trial in which a young gypsy fellow was charged with rape. The trial was held four years after the date of the offense, as he'd quickly left town after the crime was committed, and couldn't be found. He contended that at the time of the offense he was under the age of sixteen — and so couldn't be tried as an adult.

"His mother testified that he wasn't born in 1960, as the accused himself had stated, but in 1962, which would have made him a juvenile at the time of the crime. She was proud of being a gypsy and in the course of her testimony she admitted that she'd practiced witchcraft on two occasions in Ontario.

"At the end of the trial I found the accused guilty and said, in effect, that his mother was a liar. Then I set the case over for psychiatric assessment before sentencing.

"A few minutes later, a security guard told me that the accused's mother was in the courtroom and was sticking pins in a doll that bore a striking resemblance to me. He said it was a voodoo doll and she was putting a curse on me.

"I laughed and thought nothing of it. But four days later, I couldn't get out of bed. My back had completely gone out on me.

"I concluded that this was too much of a coincidence, and a few days later, after I'd imposed a sentence of six years, I spoke to the security guard again, told him what had happened to me and suggested that he try to get the doll back from the mother.

"'There could be some money in it for you,' I said.

"'How's that, Your Lordship?' the guard asked.

"'Well,' I replied, 'I told my wife all about this and her eyes lit up and she said: I've just *gotta* have that doll!'"

It's crucial for counsel to know when to shut up and sit down, and the sooner one learns this the better for one's career.

Kimberley, British Columbia, lawyer John Van Steinburg was one of the lucky ones. He learned a year or so before he was actually called to the bar — thanks to a witty and kindly judge.

A decade ago, Van Steinburg started work as an articling student in a law firm that provided free legal representation to its employees. Shortly thereafter, a young secretary was charged with a minor offense and he was the designated defender.

"Upon review of the case," John writes, "it immediately became apparent that the charge had little, if any, merit. But I resolved to really strut my stuff — particularly because the accused and all her witnesses were young ladies of my acquaintance, and I wanted to impress them.

"Accordingly, I prepared a submission of great brilliance, incorporating authorities all the way back to Lord Coke in the 1500s, as well as numerous classical and biblical references.

"On the day of the trial, I appeared before a veteran jurist, His Honor Judge David Lunn of the Provincial Court of British Columbia. Judge Lunn had seen and heard it all — many, many times.

"Fortunately for my client — but to my chagrin — my cross-examination of the Crown's witnesses revealed that no offense had been committed, and so Judge Lunn threw the case out before I could open for the defense.

"I was nonplussed. Not only had I put in hours of work, I also had a full gallery of young ladies hanging on my every word. I looked up at the judge and asked, 'Don't you want to hear my submissions?' and he immediately shot back, 'Not unless you want me to change my mind!'"

From time to time, judges have words of advice for witnesses and lawyers. Take, for example, the legendary Mr. Justice George Walsh of the Supreme Court of Ontario. In an annulment case tried by him thirty-plus years ago, the court reporter preserved this gem for posterity:

HIS LORDSHIP: On your wedding night you found out it was only a little thing?"
PLAINTIFF: Yes, My Lord.

HIS LORDSHIP: Well, you should have had a trial run.
PLAINTIFF: I guess I should have.

Garry K. Braund, Q.C., of Toronto, always breaks up when he recalls the day, back in the early 1960s, when Magistrate P. J. Bolsby had some advice for lawyer Mannie Frankel.

The now-deceased Frankel, a fixture in Toronto's criminal courts for forty years, often injected himself, uninvited, into cases where the accused had no lawyer.

"I appear as a "friend of the court," he'd say, reciting an age-old phrase. A friend of the court" — *amicus curiae*, if you prefer Latin — is a person, not necessarily a lawyer, who intervenes in a trial to bring certain matters to the attention of the court.

When it came to butting in, Mannie was bilingual. Sometimes he spoke the magic words in Latin. Other times he stuck to English. He was so versatile that occasionally he used both versions in the same intervention, as in: "As *amicus curiae*, Your Worship, I appear as a friend of the court." By executing such a verbal double-play, he made it clear that he was there to play hardball.

This was the kind of spunk that inspired some of Mannie's colleagues to bestow upon him a slogan he did not seek but must have cherished: "If they've got you by the ankle, yell for Frankel!"

Well, anyway, one memorable day — the day Garry Braund recalls so fondly — Mannie went on a veritable rampage.

"I appear as a friend of the court," he announced after Magistrate Bolsby had fined a man and given him the option to serve thirty days in jail.

"Yes, Mr. Frankel, what's the problem?" sighed His Worship.

"You didn't give that man fifteen days to pay."

"All right. An oversight. Fifteen days to pay."

That's the way it went for the next few hours — friend of the court this, *amicus curiae* that. Etcetera. Etcetera. Mannie popped up so often he was well-nigh pooped.

Then Magistrate Bolsby, who'd had it up to here, did some intervening of his own.

"Mr. Frankel," he said, "I have some advice for you."

"Yes, Your Worship?"

"Keep your friendship to yourself!"

Provincial Court Judge C. Emerson Perkins of Chatham, Ontario, sends this reminiscence on the subject of one-upmanship:

"The Honorable W. Ross Macdonald had just retired as lieutenant-governor of Ontario and his hometown of Brantford was holding a dinner in his honor on a Friday evening. Harold Stafford, Q.C., the chairman of the Ontario section of the Liberal caucus under Pierre Trudeau, had been delegated to represent the prime minister and the governor-general at this dinner.

"On the Monday preceding that Friday, Mr. Stafford commenced a trial before Judge D. B. Menzies of London. The trial wasn't finished at the end of the day and Judge Menzies said that there was time on the court calendar to continue on Friday.

"To this, Mr. Stafford said, 'Your Honor, I can't be here on Friday,' and with a note of some pride in his voice he added, 'On that day I will be in Brantford representing the prime minister and the governor-general of Canada.' To which Judge Menzies replied, 'That is all very impressive, Mr. Stafford, but let me remind you that on that Friday I will be here in London, in this court, representing Her Majesty the Queen.'"

A dab or two of judicial humor can work wonders in a courtroom — to momentarily relieve boredom, to snap the sometimes unbearable tension, to put a frightened witness at ease.

Mr. Justice Raymond J. Halley, of the Supreme Court of Newfoundland, recalls a case that had little boredom, plenty of tension, and a mighty scared little girl in the witness box. Fortunately, it also had a kindly, witty judge.

The young lass had been sexually assaulted near her home in Happy Valley, Labrador, not far from a United States air base. Two U.S. servicemen were arrested and charged, but feelings ran so high in the area that the defense obtained an order changing the place of trial to the city of St. John's in mainland Newfoundland.

Mr. Justice James D. Higgins presided at the trial, which was held in a courtroom jammed to the gunwales with media representatives and spectators. The girl, far from home and overawed by the crowd and the excitement, was terrified as she was sworn in as the first witness. On the front of the witness box, a pair of microphones stuck out at an angle and nearly poked her in the eye.

"Will you please give us your name?" the Crown Attorney asked.

There was no answer.

"Could we have your name, please?"

Again, no reply.

Mr. Justice Higgins gently nudged the girl into stating her name, age and address, and then he said, "My dear, why don't you tell us now what happened?"

The girl put her hands over the microphones and turned to the judge and asked, with great concern, "Is this on radio?"

She smiled when she heard His Lordship's soft reply:

"Oh, no, my dear, we couldn't get a sponsor."

Donald J. Welbourn, a lawyer who practices in Claresholm, Alberta, reports as follows:

"The rarefied atmosphere of the Alberta Court of Appeal seldom admits much humor. But occasionally a judicial pun will prevail.

"A deaf man was convicted of assaulting his equally deaf wife during a heated argument. After a lengthy appeal presentation, which obliged the court to use an interpreter, the husband's appeal against conviction was granted and the Crown's cross-appeal dismissed.

"As the husband and wife, now reconciled, left the courtroom, gesticulating happily to each other, the Chief Justice was heard to admonish them both: 'Go and sign no more!'"

Don did so well with that yarn I invited him back for an encore:

"The plaintiff, a determined lady of rather awesome dimensions but of poor command of the English language, was being cross-examined by junior counsel with the aid of a blackboard diagram in a pedestrian-crossing case.

"The legendary Mr. Justice Harold Riley, late of the Alberta Court of Queen's Bench, was presiding. Some of the dialogue between the lawyer and the witness went like this:

LAWYER: Show me where in the cross-walk you were hit, madam.
WITNESS: Here (*pointing to an ample buttock*).
LAWYER: I mean where on the diagram were you hit?
WITNESS: Not hit on the diagram. Hit *here*! (*again indicating her buttock*).

"Counsel paused, frustrated, and the judge interjected kindly: 'Just show me where the injury took place, madam.'

"At which invitation the plaintiff raised her skirts and displayed to the court her magnificent unclad posterior, one side of which still bore obvious bruising.

"As the junior counsel involved, I had the presence of mind to promptly sit down.

"In finding my client negligent, Mr. Justice Riley, no mean punster, solemnly stated for the record: 'The bare facts of this case have been well demonstrated by the plaintiff, and in the end she shall have her judgment.'"

Provincial Court Judge C. J. Cannon of Toronto has a story about one of his colleagues, Judge Donald F. Graham:

"Judge Graham, who's been on the bench for thirty-three years, has a habit of rocking back in his chair as he listens to lawyers making submissions. One day, while he was doing this, the chair tipped over and His Honor disappeared from view.

"Defense counsel stopped in mid-sentence, and a hush spread over the courtroom. Then a seemingly disembodied voice wafted up from below the bench, ringing loud and clear: 'Keep talking, counsel, I can still hear you!'"

Judge Cannon's back for seconds. This time he's snitching on a *former* colleague, Thomas R. Swabey, who sat on the Provincial Court in Ottawa for about a decade but now practices law in Cornwall, Ontario. This yarn is as authentic as they come because Judge Cannon got it from Tom Swabey himself:

"Judge Swabey was hearing a case involving an alleged breach of a city bylaw and the woman in the witness box prefaced almost every one of her answers with the same string of words: 'May the good Lord strike me dead with lightning if I'm not telling the truth.'

"After hearing this six or seven times, Judge Swabey leaned forward and said to the woman, 'I wonder if you'd do something for me.'

"'Certainly, Your Honor,' she said. 'What's that?'

"'Would you mind moving farther away from me?' asked the judge. 'I don't want to get injured or killed when the bolt of lightning strikes!'"

Contrary to popular belief, few judges get their jollies sentencing people. A great many judges hate it and agonize over it. A wide variety of factors, some subtle and some not so subtle, can come into play. If you're fair, you don't want to be too hard. But you don't want to be too soft, either. There should probably be a full-time, always-on-call patron saint of judges.

Hard or soft, just about everybody in the judgin' business would agree that, when it comes to sentencing folks, it helps a whole lot if you have some kind of an idea of what you're doing.

Toronto criminal lawyer Roderick G. MacGregor recalls hearing a rookie judge, a mite unsure of himself, sentencing a man for theft.

"I've heard all the evidence and I've listened carefully to counsel's submissions," he told the bloke in the dock, "and I hereby sentence you to two months . . . no, make that years."

5

THE JUDGE WHO KNEW EVERYTHING

TRUTH IS STRANGER THAN FICTION. FICTION IS OBLIGED TO STICK
TO POSSIBILITIES; TRUTH ISN'T.

Mark Twain

One day in the early 1960s, a young Ottawa lawyer approached a judge at a party and, excusing himself for talking shop out of season, declared that he had a professional problem.

"What's your problem?" inquired the judge.

"My Lord," the lawyer replied, "there are three uncontested divorce cases that I have on your list of trials during the current Supreme Court Assizes. Next week I'm scheduled to go deer hunting with friends and I'd appreciate it very much if I could have these three quick cases set down to be heard this week."

"I'll see if I can arrange that," said the judge. Next morning he did a bit of juggling and was able to oblige. He told the lawyer that the divorce cases would be heard Friday afternoon, starting at four o'clock. In this report, fictitious names abound.

Leblanc versus Leblanc and Lebel was the first case to be heard.

Mrs. Leblanc, an attractive young woman, had no trouble with the routine questions preceding the crucial evidence of adultery. Then her lawyer said to the judge, "My Lord, I now file the certificate of marriage and the proof of service of the writ and statement of claim on the husband, Roméo Leblanc, and the co-respondent, Jeannette Lebel."

The judge looked at the marriage certificate and said to the witness, "You were married in Sudbury?"

"Yes, sir," she replied. "In fact, you know my husband — he's the son of the owner of Leblanc Cartage."

"Oh."

"Yes, and you attended his stag party before our wedding. You remember Jeannette, daughter of your friend Pierre Lebel?"

"Uh . . . uh . . . yes," sputtered the judge.

"Well," the woman continued, "her father must have told you that his daughter Jeannette is living with my husband in Ottawa."

"Uh . . . uh," His Lordship said softly, fearful that it would appear that he — and not just Mrs. Leblanc — was giving evidence.

When Mrs. Leblanc was finished testifying, her sister confirmed in the witness box that Roméo and Jeannette were living as man and wife and the judge granted a "decree *nisi*" — a preliminary divorce decree that would be made final in a few months. Then he told the court clerk, rather hurriedly, "Call the next case."

The next case was *Moulton versus Moulton and Sanchez*. After the lawyer had filed documents, he called his client, the husband, who testified that a few months earlier his wife had been on the verge of a nervous breakdown and, with his blessing, she and their young daughter had a two-week vacation in Mexico.

Mrs. Moulton returned, enthralled by her trip and restored to health. For the next month, her husband said, she talked a great deal about Mexico and declared that she just *had* to go back there, the sooner the better. Her husband told her to banish the thought from her mind because family finances wouldn't permit it.

A few days later, Mr. Moulton came home from work and found that his wife and daughter had vanished. For several months there was no news of their whereabouts. Then Mrs. Moulton's sister showed Mr. Moulton a letter she'd received from his wife. It was posted in a city in Mexico called Cuernavaca and it stated that she was living with a Mexican man, was extremely happy, and would never return to Canada.

The young lawyer was informed of these sad developments and arranged for a private investigator to serve divorce papers in Cuernavaca.

A few months later, back in Ottawa, the investigator testified: "I had no information as to where Mrs. Moulton lived in Cuernavaca. I consulted a local lawyer and he told me that most people go to the 'Centro' where the post office is, and most of the shops. So I sat at a sidewalk table of a restaurant, well in view of the park, post office and shops. I'm sorry, My Lord, I don't remember the name of the restaurant."

"Would it be the Restaurante Universale?" His Lordship asked.

"Yes, that's it," the man said, somewhat surprised.

"I sat there at the table for two days," the investigator continued, "and I had a picture of her in front of me at all times. I figured that Mrs. Moulton, being blonde, would be easy to distinguish from the natives. Then, on the second day, I saw her and a child walking across the square with a Mexican man.

"I approached her, told her who I was, and stated the purpose of my trip. She was very friendly and agreed to come with me to the office of the lawyer I had consulted. When we were there, I served the divorce papers, in the presence of the lawyer, and he dictated a document — a certificate — in Spanish."

"Here is that certificate, My Lord," said Mr. Moulton's lawyer, "and I have a translation as well."

"Never mind," said the judge. "I'm conversant with that language." He read the document carefully, then said to the witness, "Continue."

"Well, after that," said the detective, "Mrs. Moulton and the man — Henrique Sanchez — kindly invited me to go to their home. I agreed, and they drove me to a small but comfortable house. I forget the name of that part of the city. We went almost to the end of the main street, then . . ."

"That is Calle Guerrero," the judge interjected.

"That's it!" said the witness, flabbergasted. "We went up the hill on the flank of the mountain to an area . . . I'm sorry, I forget the name."

"Would it be Fraccionamento Loma Sol?" asked the judge.

"Yes, now I remember, that's the name they mentioned," the

witness replied, with a quizzical look.

A few minutes later, the judge granted the decree *nisi* and then the clerk called the last of the three cases to be presented by the lawyer — *Smith versus Smith and Jones.*

"My Lord, this is also an uncontested action," the lawyer began. "The defendants are living together, here in Ottawa."

The plaintiff husband entered the witness box and, touching all the bases, quickly established the marriage, the separation, and all other essential facts. He then gave way to the next witness, a private detective named Benjamin A. Proulx.

"I'd been given this picture of the wife and the address where these parties were supposed to live," Mr. Proulx told the court.

"On the day in question, I stationed myself at the corner of Dalhousie and Rideau Streets — at the door of the Larocque store — at about 4:30 P.M. I had a clear view of the door across the street — number 176½ Rideau Street. At about 5:30 P.M., I saw this couple enter that doorway. I recognized the woman from the picture I had."

"Then what did you do?" asked the lawyer.

"I went home. I didn't follow them because I figured that at that hour the man would say he was only visiting the woman. I came back to 176½ Rideau at 11:30 P.M. I went up the staircase and down the hallway a few feet to the first door, Apartment Number One."

"Just a moment, witness!" said the judge. "You couldn't go down the hallway that easily. At the top of the stairs there's a door, and that door is locked after seven o'clock at night. Did you have a key?"

"I beg your pardon, sir," said the embarrassed witness. "You're quite right. I forgot to tell you that a few minutes after I saw the couple, I went into the building, identified myself to the superintendent, told him I had something important to deliver to Apartment Number One later in the evening, and he said he'd leave the door unlocked until midnight."

Mr. Proulx said he knocked at the door of the apartment and after several minutes a man in pajamas opened the door.

"I asked to speak to Mrs. Smith," he continued. "The man said,

'She's in bed. What do you want?' I told him a divorce action had been started against Mrs. Smith and asked if he'd let me in to discuss the matter privately.

"He opened the door wide and I entered the apartment. Inside, there was a door on the right to, I think, a bedroom . . ."

"No!" snapped the judge.

The witness looked aghast.

"Let me tell you, Mr. Proulx, you're *wrong*! The door to that bedroom is on the *left* side! I *know*!"

"You're correct, My Lord," gulped the startled witness. "Once again, you're right!"

Everything went well from then on. The judge granted the divorce and the lawyer thanked him for accommodating him and then headed off for the woods.

A few days after he'd returned from his hunting trip, the lawyer bumped into the judge and said, "A lady who was in court and heard the three trials came up to me as I was leaving and asked, 'Does that judge know *everything*?'"

Maybe it's time to let the lady in on a few things:

The judge was Mr. Justice Leo Albert Landreville and the lawyer was Dan Chilcott — the same Dan Chilcott who, a quarter-century later, became treasurer of the Law Society of Upper Canada and shortly thereafter a Justice of the Supreme Court of Ontario. For many years after Mr. Justice Landreville left the bench, he and Chilcott were law partners.

The puzzled woman might have known the names of the judge and the lawyer, but she likely did *not* know that: (a) Leo Landreville lived in Sudbury for twenty-five years and had been the mayor of that city; (b) Landreville had a second home for several years — in Cuernavaca, Mexico; and (c) Landreville grew up in the building the detective staked out on Rideau Street.

"My father owned that building," Leo Landreville said recently, after favoring me with this story. "In fact, the bedroom where the adultery took place used to be my parents' bedroom!"

Life goes on and "the long arm of coincidence" reaches out in all directions — sometimes to caress our funnybones.

6

They Gave At The Office

WORK IS MUCH MORE FUN THAN FUN.

Noel Coward

Surely you jest, Mr. Coward.

You can't be suggesting that work is always a hoot. You must be aware, sir, that every occupation has its fair share of boredom and drudgery. Did all those witty words you wrote just tumble onto the page? Did you never sit staring at blank paper until your eyeballs receded into your skull? Did merriment accompany your every working moment?

Now if what you mean is that some jobs are more likely to spark the odd moment of fun than others, I'm with you all the way. Folks who are involved in such lines of employment are fortunate indeed, for they know that at least every now and then a fleeting moment of fun will come to brighten their day. That's the way it is in the world of law.

The courtroom isn't the only place in the legal firmament where levity lurks, you know. Sometimes law offices and court offices are pretty jolly joints, too, what with lawyers, judges, clients, secretaries, and others inducing a case of the giggles. The work that's performed in such establishments is pressure-packed and oh-so-serious, and when someone mercifully snaps the tension, for however short a time, everyone feels good all over and returns to the job refreshed.

This chapter is about people who brought the precious gift of laughter into the workplace — people who truly "gave at the office."

We begin our tour at the office of Toronto lawyer Murray D. Silverberg. Recently I received letters from Murray and one of his secretaries — letters that raise the sneaking suspicion that at the Silverberg spread it's just one laugh after another.

The first to take typewriter in hand was secretary Laurie Revesz, who filed this report:

"Due to the need for part-time typing and general office help, our office hired a secretary with no previous legal experience. She was a reliable, accurate typist who was willing to learn real estate law.

"After a few weeks she was quite at ease in preparing statements of adjustment for sale transactions. Although she was accurate in her calculations on such adjustments, I still wonder if she fully comprehended the meaning of the vendor's adjustment for interest for the unadvanced portion of a mortgage. The adjustment is made when a purchaser takes over the seller's mortgage payments.

"Our adjustment in this regard is calculated for the period 'from closing to I.A.D.' (short for 'Interest Adjustment Date').

"When questioned on the telephone by the lawyer acting for the purchaser as to why there appeared a credit to the vendor for such interest adjustment, she confidently replied: 'That credit is an adjustment due by the purchaser for her I.U.D.'"

Still reeling from the revelation that real estate deals involved such intimate matters, I opened the mail a few days later and there was another letter about the same madcap office — this one from the boss himself.

"I was just opening up my office as a new sole practitioner," he began. "I sublet space from a small firm, which included use of all their office equipment. In an effort to save salary overhead, I hired a very young, inexperienced secretary who had never worked in an office before.

"One day, a couple of months after opening for business, I was wandering around the office when, for no particular reason, I glanced in the tray which contained my outgoing correspondence. One of the secretary's responsibilities was applying the postage to the mail, using the firm's postage meter.

"When I saw the envelopes on top of the outgoing stack, I detected something strange about the postage. I went through the balance of the mail and discovered it had been posted in the same manner.

"I asked the secretary if she had applied the postage. She advised that she had, and she also confirmed that she had always done my mail in the same way.

"Little did I realize how my cost-saving scheme of hiring an inexperienced secretary would pay such quick dividends.

"The postage on all my letters for the past two months had been stamped, not with a postage meter, but with a cheque-writing machine!"

Jay Rumanek, head of a large Montreal law firm, has a heart-tugging tale about the love of a father for his son:

"As Director of the Criminal Appeals Section of the Montreal Legal Aid Bureau, I am required to examine applications for legal aid in appeal, in order to determine whether or not there are grounds for appeal which might reasonably be raised before the higher courts.

"Recently, an elderly gentleman called me in connection with the case of his son who had been sentenced to life imprisonment with eligibility for parole after twenty-five years, pursuant to a conviction on a charge of first-degree murder. I told him that I would look into the case.

"Unfortunately for the convicted man, it was an open-and-shut case in which the judge's instructions to the jury had been impeccable. My study of the case, under the circumstances, did not take very long, and when the father called back a few days later I regretfully reported to him that there was nothing that could be done for his son.

"'Oh, well, okay,' the man replied, 'tell him to call me when he gets out.'"

Jay also reports that a prisoner requesting legal aid wrote to him from a maximum-security penitentiary and began his letter thusly: "Dear Mr. Rumanek, I am taking advantage of a few free moments to write to you . . ."

Judge James P. Felstiner, of the Provincial Court (Family Division) in Toronto, received a letter from a thirteen-year-old girl who'd been ordered to do forty hours of community service work as penance for her sins. In her letter to the court, she was expected to describe the services she'd performed for her community and state what she learned from the whole exercise. This is what she wrote:

"Dear your honor — I am just writing to tell you that I have finished my commity work. I found it quite hard because I usally like to go outside a lot but I had to stay in and commity work. The thing I liked best about it was the Bingo."

Daniel Lyon, lawyer for a Toronto-based film-production company, tells about a memorable letter that, uh, sent him reeling.

"Entertainment law can be quite entertaining," Dan writes. "We frequently have occasion to negotiate agreements with American studios, and one of the common 'boiler plate' issues concerns whose laws should govern in the interpretation of the contract.

"A recent letter of comments to us from the legal department of a major international supplier of television programming contained a paragraph which was surprisingly deficient in both law and geography. It said: 'Governing laws should be New York. It also seems to make sense that the parties should agree to jurisdiction and venue in New York since New York is very roughly the mid-point between Quebec and Los Angeles.'

"We resisted the temptation to enclose a map of North America with our reply."

Toronto lawyer Gordon I. Kirke, a specialist in sports and entertainment law, tells about a client who shares the Boy Scout belief that one should always "Be Prepared." All right, Gord, let's have the facts:

"I was representing a client involved in the business of sports.

He came to my office to prepare for a meeting we were to have later that day.

"During our preparatory meeting, my client asked me if I thought that the other lawyer in the transaction was dull-witted. I tried to defend my learned friend but my client exclaimed, 'My God! If there were a Stupidity Olympics, that lawyer would be the Nadia Comaneci!'

"Later that same day, my client and I attended the meeting with the other party to the transaction and his lawyer. Sure enough, during the course of the meeting the lawyer came out with a totally incomprehensible and inappropriate comment.

"Immediately, my client reached into his briefcase and extracted two cards which he held out over his head, each proclaiming: '9.5.'"

Saskatoon lawyer Jim Biss knows that, when you're looking for a chuckle, sometimes things go better with — a chattel mortgage.

"I recently received instructions to prepare chattel security," he writes. "The borrower gave me a handwritten list of chattels that were to be mortgaged in the document. Included on that list was this item: 'one cock machine.'

"I haven't quite figured out how we would take enforcement proceedings and, in particular, how we would seize it."

One day, not so long ago, a Western judge was chatting in his office with an old friend who'd dropped in to see him. They got to talking about the pros and cons of various occupations and His Honor remarked, "The problem with being a judge is that you deal with the dregs of society."

"And their clients, too," quipped his friend.

Legal secretary Barbara Tuck, of Thornhill, Ontario, wrote to me recently to "contribute my one and only story." It was a winner, as most secretaries would probably agree:

"I used to work for an older lawyer who liked to have his secretary bring him coffee every morning, which I did gladly.

"Well, one morning I was a bit slow with it and after a few minutes my boss said, 'Good morning, Barbara. How about a cup of coffee?' To which I replied, 'No, thanks, Mr. Robertson, I've already had one.'"

And, speaking of piping-hot beverages, Provincial Court Judge James A. Fontana files this report from the nation's capital:

"One day in 1989, in the cafeteria of the new Ottawa Court House, the very formal and courteous defense lawyer, Peter Beach, who used to be a barrister in England, was walking back from the counter, balancing his tray. He was somehow jostled and spilled a pot of tea over the elegantly clad Miss Sharon Rosenberg, also a defense lawyer, who was dining with a group of other lawyers.

"Peter apologized profusely, offering to assist Miss Rosenberg and pay for the dry-cleaning. She would have none of it, thanked Peter and told him not to worry about it.

"When Miss Rosenberg returned to her office a little later that afternoon she was pleasantly surprised to find on her desk a dozen long-stemmed roses from Peter and a card of apology. She picked up the phone and called Peter's office to thank him. Peter was not in, his secretary said, but was there any message?

"'Tell Peter he can spill tea on me any time,' said Miss Rosenberg.

"There was a long silence on the phone.

"'Are you sure you want me to tell Mr. Beach that?' the secretary asked, perplexed.

"'Exactly that. He'll know what it means. Be sure that he gets the message.'

"'If you say so, Miss Rosenberg,' said the ever-obedient secretary.

"Shortly after this Peter returned to his office to find a phone message on his desk, which said: 'Tell Peter he can still pee on me any time.'"

St. John's, Newfoundland, lawyer William H. Goodridge sent me a memorandum pertaining to a crisis that sprang up one day, in the late 1960s, in the office of the law firm he's associated with. The memo, written by a secretary, reads as follows:

"A former female employee of the firm was filling in as receptionist when a male client arrived for an appointment.

"After he gave his name he asked the receptionist if he could use the lavatory. She hesitated a moment (not knowing the meaning of the word *lavatory* and thinking it might be the library) and replied that the lavatory was in use. The client said that was all right, he would wait.

"The receptionist said, 'Well, Mr. Reid, our law student, is there and he will probably be there all day because he doesn't have an office.'

"The client frowned and said, 'I really need to use the lavatory soon.'

"The receptionist, sensing something was amiss and becoming flustered, replied, 'You really cannot go there because Mr. Reid uses it all the time and it isn't very large, and sometimes our other student, Mr. Wells, is there with him.'

"The client had become by this time very agitated and he roared, 'Lady, do you have a *bathroom*?' The receptionist, very meekly, said, 'Yes, up the stairs.'"

In 1989, Dorothy Turcotte, a retired court official who lives in Grimsby, Ontario, sent me this vivid recollection of how things were down at the office, back in the good old days:

"In the late 1940s, I worked in the Court Clerk's office at Central Police Station in Hamilton. One of the staff in our office was a uniformed policeman, Sergeant Jackson, who attended court regularly. He was a tough-looking bird with small steel-rimmed glasses and a shaved head. Handcuffs routinely dangled from his back pocket.

"Sergeant Jackson always kept a box of cigars in the bottom drawer of his desk, and he puffed on them constantly. When the box was empty, he'd unlock the basement door, go downstairs, and reappear with a fresh box.

"One day, someone asked him why he got his cigars downstairs, instead of at the store like everyone else. Squinting through the smoke as he dragged on a fresh cigar, he replied: 'They were confiscated at a carnival. The judge told me to take them out and burn them. So that's what I'm doing — one at a time.'"

Former magistrate Hugh O'Neill, Q.C., of St. John's, has many stories about Newfoundland courts — especially the tribunals of a century or so ago. In one of several conversations I've had with him in person and by phone, Hugh told me about a caper that was pulled — with judicial sanction, yet! — back in the free-wheeling 1890s.

In a trial held on a schooner, a magistrate named Macdonnell convicted a man on a charge of smuggling a large quantity of booze into Newfoundland from the nearby island of St. Pierre. His Worship ordered that the confiscated grog be "destroyed."

But he didn't say when — or how.

In point of fact, the hooch was removed to the magistrate's office, where he and the copper who made the bust, a certain Sergeant Goodland, met regularly to "destroy" it glass by glass. "It took a year to accomplish," lawyer-historian Hugh O'Neill reports.

In a legal career that stretches back to 1933 and includes forty-two years on the bench, the aforementioned Hugh O'Neill — well into his eighties and still practicing law — has amassed memories galore.

Somehow, in one of our talks, we got onto the subject of estates and I asked him what was the most memorable provision he'd ever seen in a will. A split second later Hugh advised that the "champeen" clause was in a will that "an outport chap named John" brought into the office of a colleague. The document was the last hurrah of the fellow's recently departed daddy, and it said in part: "To my son John, I leave my commode and its contents."

People who work in law offices and courthouses occasionally get to see some pretty nasty language in wills submitted for probate. Some of it's so vicious and vengeful it's even funny — if you're not the one it was aimed at, that is.

Take, for example, the wealthy man who wrote: "To my wife I leave her lover and the knowledge I wasn't the fool she thought I was. To my son I leave the pleasure of earning a living. For twenty-five years he thought the pleasure was mine, but he was mistaken. To my valet I leave the clothes he has been stealing from me regularly for ten years, also the fur coat he wore last winter while I was in Palm Beach. To my chauffeur I leave my cars. He has almost ruined them and I want him to have the satisfaction of finishing the job."

The preceding outburst seems almost tame when compared with a testamentary tirade contained in a will that Toronto lawyer Kenneth Picov came across recently. One paragraph of said document — with names changed — had this to say:

"To my daughter Mary Smith the sum of one dollar. To my son-in-law John Robert Smith the sum of one dollar and nineteen cents, or such amount as necessary to purchase sufficient rat poison to remove the God-given life from his vile, filthy body."

Fortunately, not everyone who makes a will feels the way that gent did. In a great many such documents, generosity abounds.

Take, for example, a will that was submitted for probate in Cayuga, Ontario, in 1989. As soon as Judge Paul Forestell and his staff spotted paragraph 3 (e) thereof they knew that the deceased was either a man of unbridled generosity or a dude who knew diddly-squat about desks. It said: "To deliver to my son, John Paul Jones, for his own use absolutely, my secretary."

Vernon, British Columbia, lawyer R. S. Adams tells about a client who left this vale of tears on a note of generosity. As a postscript to his will, the client scribbled a note that read as follows:

> Dec. 16 1982
> Last Request
> No funeral No coffin
> Just put in sack and Creemate
> No Preacher Just take a Bottle of whisky
> and in vite all Enemies in.

A will has been described as "a device for splitting heirs." In the 1970s, a Dallas woman found a dandy new way of going about it — as this short, snappy news story attests:

"Emma Warren, an 88-year-old widow, wanted to know whether

her relatives deserved to inherit her fortune. She instructed her lawyers to send out telegrams advising the family of her death and inviting them to a funeral tea at her home.

"From a hiding place, she monitored the conversation of the relatives. The next day, all were cut from Mrs. Warren's will except two who spoke kindly of her."

I'm deeply indebted to another Texan for my all-time favorite will. It was composed by a farmer named Herman Oberweiss, a fellow who wanted the whole wide world to know just what he thought of his brother, Oscar. Here's Herman's last will and testament, exactly as he writ it:

"I am writing of my will mineself that des lawyir want he should have so much money he ask to many answers about the family. First think i want done i don't want my brother Oscar to get a god dam thing. I got he is a musser he done me out of four dollars fourteen years since.

"I want it that Hilda my sister she gets the north sixtie akers of at where I am homing it now i bet she dont get that loafer husband of hers to brake twenty akers next ploughing. She cant have it if she lets Oscar live on it i want it should have it back if she does.

"Tell mama that six hundret dollars she has been looking for ten years is berried from the bakhouse behind about ten foot down. She is better lett little Frederick do the digging and count it when he comes up.

"Pastor Licknitz can have three hundret dollars if he kisses the book he won't preach no more dumhead talks about politks. He should a roof put on the meeting house with the elders should the bills look at.

"Mama should the rest get but i want it so that Adolph should tell her what not she should do so no more slick irishers sell her vaken cleaner they noise like hell and a broom dont cost so much.

"I want it that mine brother Adolph be my executor and i want it that the judge should pleese make Adolph plenty bond put up and watch him like hell. Adolph is a good business man but only a dumkoph would trust him with a busted pfennig.

"I want dam sure that schleimiel Oscar dont nothing get tell Adolph he can have a hundret dollars if he prove to judge Oscar dont get nothing. That dam sure fix Oscar."

Zillions of folks state in their wills that their bodies are to be cremated and the ashes strewn over some favorite spot on the globe that had never failed in the past to provide them with many marvelous memories. One such romantic was an otherwise hard-bitten customer, the great writer Damon Runyon, who instructed his executor to scatter his ashes over his beloved Broadway.

Another fellow, a frustrated golfer, helped himself to a posthumous giggle by taking a totally different approach. He provided in his will that his ashes were to be placed in a certain sandtrap that his ball had frequented with maddening regularity.

D. James Ramsay, a lawyer in Kelowna, British Columbia, tells of a client who evoked instantaneous memories of the dearly departed Gracie Allen.

Take us home, Jim:

"Some years ago, while taking instructions from a young couple for preparation of their wills, the subject of burial wishes arose.

"The husband told me that they both wished to be cremated, with the ashes being sprinkled over Kalamalka Lake in the Okanagan Valley of British Columbia.

"At that point, his wife interrupted and said, 'Oh, no, dear, that won't do — I can't swim!'"

7

BAKER VERSUS McPHEE

A GOOD AND WHOLESOME THING IS A LITTLE HARMLESS FUN IN
THIS WORLD; IT TONES A BODY UP AND KEEPS HIM HUMAN AND
PREVENTS HIM FROM SOURING.

Mark Twain

It's a pretty safe bet that if people had more honest-to-God fun
than they seem to have these days, there'd be a lot less "burnout"
— and many fewer slipped trolleys — in this crazy old world of
ours. We're talking good, old-fashioned fun — especially the kind
of merriment that folks manufacture, free of charge, themselves.

Take lawyers, for example. Lawyers used to have a lot of fun,
even while at work. Some of them still do, of course, but most have
become *sooooo* serious that they rarely stop to smell the flowers.

That's not the way it was with "Tobey" Jones and "Laddy"
Forsyth, a couple of learned gentlemen in my hometown of
Halifax, Nova Scotia, who loved to horse around on occasion.
They were full-time lawyers and part-time poets, and in 1922
they had a jolly time indeed with a dispute that involved eighteen
dollars and change.

I refer to the celebrated case of *Baker versus McPhee*, the
outcome of which no one seems to know — or care. If someone
recalls the result I'd welcome the "news," but it's of no great
importance. What matters most is the *fun* that was fomented by
the barrister-bards you're about to meet.

Baker, the plaintiff, was represented by Owen Bell Jones, an eminent lawyer whose nickname was "Tobey." Jones, who was called to the bar of Nova Scotia in 1914, served overseas in World War I and was discharged with the rank of major. Acting for the defendant was Lionel A. Forsyth, a.k.a. "Laddy." Forsyth became a lawyer in 1918. He practiced for a while in Windsor, Nova Scotia, then set up shop in Halifax, and later in Montreal. After a distinguished career at the bar he became president of the Dominion Steel and Coal Corporation.

The focal point of this titanic legal tussle was a dilapidated shay — a two-wheel carriage — that Baker left with McPhee for repairs. In such a situation, the law describes Baker as the "bailor" and McPhee as the "bailee." A bailee must take care of goods entrusted to him.

Now, without further ado, here are some letters that Tobey and Laddy dashed off to each other about their *cause célèbre*:

August 30th, 1922

L. A. Forsyth, Esq.
Barrister
Halifax, N.S.

Baker vs. McPhee

Dear Sir:

> I note what you say
> Regarding the shay
> That Mr. McPhee has allowed to decay,
> And also the tender
> You asked us to render,
> But my client says
> That McPhee didn't mend 'er,
> But rather, says he, that Mr. McPhee
> Neglected his duty as Baker's bailee.
> The carriage entrusted to him is now busted;
> The top's all ripped and the lamps are all rusted.

McPhee further claims
That, speaking of names,
My Mr. Baker is Jacob, not James.
In this I agree with Mr. McPhee
But don't think it matters materially.

In brief, Baker's willing,
Sans backing and filling,
To pay for the wheels at the rate McPhee's billing,
Provided McPhee will also agree
To fix up the top and the lamps for him free.

Yours truly,
Owen B. Jones

August 30th, 1922

Owen B. Jones, Esq.
Barrister, etc.
Halifax, N.S.

<u>Re: Baker vs. McPhee</u>

Dear Sir:

Your letter received and if Baker's believed
It might be admitted he's rightly aggrieved,
But as soon as we saw
That your statement of law
When applied to the facts
Appeared somewhat raw
We spoke to McPhee
And undoubtedly he
Is not, as you state,
In default as bailee.

On the question of name,
Be it said to his shame,
Your client's been playing a fraudulent game.
The Bankruptcy Act,
As a matter of fact,
Would penalize him for the candor he lacked.
Section 99 (d), you must frankly agree,
Was plainly intended for just such as he.
And Mr. McPhee says that Faulkner, Trustee,
Could also proceed under 99 (d).

To the Bankruptcy Court we shall have to resort
If you care to proceed with your action in Court.
But make no mistake,
If such action you take,
It will not be McPhee that you break.
As of course you expected
Your offer's rejected
And we'll try to see
That McPhee is protected.
So if in the end
A summons you send
We undertake to appear and defend.

                        Yours very truly,
                        L. A. Forsyth

                                    August 31st, 1922

Lionel A. Forsyth, Esq.
Barrister, etc.
Halifax, N.S.
                    Re: Baker vs. McPhee
Dear Sir:

    Were it not for the fact
    That with great lack of tact

You've hinted at fraud
In the client I've backed,
I'd feel much inclined
To make up my mind
To issue a summons, as I had designed.
But Baker's good breeding
Now bids him take heeding
To mix not with men who resort to such pleading.

Indeed, Mr. Baker will swear by his Maker
That Mr. McPhee is a bit of a faker.
He clamors and hollers for eighteen-odd dollars
And when we default, why our buggy he collars.
While we say politely he's not acting rightly,
We'll pay him in full when the buggy's made sightly.

I note that you say my law's all astray;
Now what will their Lordships the Justices say?
I'll wager a lot they'll wax pretty hot
On hearing our buggy's all gone to pot.
But surely McPhee will not want to see
A judgment recorded against him by me.

Be pleased to explain to McPhee once again
That we want a top that will keep out the rain.
And tell him, I pray, we'd rather the shay
Had lamps on the side to light up the way.
It's quite asininal, my learned friend Lionel,
To quibble at length over this; this is final.

Yours truly,
Owen B. Jones

8

THE PEOPLE'S COURT

LET JUSTICE BE DONE, THOUGH THE HEAVENS FALL!

The Earl of Mansfield (1705-1793)

Move over, Judge Wopner.

Shortly after he was appointed to the County Court at Toronto in 1971, Judge Ray Stortini was in Small Claims Court — then called Division Court — presiding over a lawsuit with two pairs of pants.

"A tailor on Spadina Avenue was offering two custom-made suits for the price of one," His Honor recalls. "A father and son decided to take advantage of the offer and ordered a suit for each of them. When the suits were finished, the son picked up his suit. However, the father didn't like the fit of his suit and refused to pay the tailor.

"At the trial, the tailor produced the suit and insisted that there was nothing wrong with it. The customer was equally insistent that the suit did not fit him properly.

"I ordered the customer to take the suit to the men's room and put it on. On his return I could see no fitting problems, although I am not a sartorial expert. I asked his son if he saw anything wrong and the honest lad replied in the negative.

"There was a rather large group of people in the courtroom and I asked them for their opinion. There was an immediate clapping of hands and a very definite indication that the suit fitted the man perfectly. Whereupon there was judgment for the tailor for the unpaid balance.

"Small Claims Court is a *People's* Court."

It certainly is.

All the Canadian provinces and territories have Small Claims Courts, though some go by a different name. They're courts where people can sue for relatively small amounts of money, usually up to a thousand dollars, and, with or without a lawyer, can have their cases heard by a legally trained person within a few weeks or months of the commencement of hostilities. They're inexpensive and much more informal than the higher courts, and I'm pleased to say that on occasion this informality breeds laughter, which is, of course, very good for body and soul.

There's no end to the things that people will sue over in Small Claims Court. Toronto lawyer Steven C. Gaon supplies some proof thereof:

"A few years ago, when I was an articled law student in Ottawa, I had a very silly Small Claims action. My client, a bicycle courier, was not the brightest fellow in the world.

"He came into my office one day and showed me a Statement of Claim that had been served on him. His former fiancée was suing him for half the cost of the wedding that never took place. In her lawsuit she alleged that she'd been jilted by my client and asked to be reimbursed for half the cost of her wedding dress, bridesmaids' dresses, disc-jockey fees, down-payment on the reception hall, and various other incidentals.

"I sat down with my client and tried to sort out the facts. First he told me that he bought his fiancée a ring, and that it cost $1,300. I said to myself, Perfect! We'll counterclaim for the cost of the ring!

"Then he told me something that I felt would turn out to be a vital piece of evidence at the trial. Apparently my client's parents and his fiancée's parents were riding in a car together, several months before the wedding date, and the intended bride's mother said to my client's mother, 'If my daughter sleeps with your son before the wedding, we won't pay a dime towards the cost of the wedding. Otherwise, we will pay for everything but the tuxedos.'

"I figured that this was proof that the woman's parents agreed to pay for the wedding and that my client had never agreed to do so. I could hardly wait to cross-examine the fiancée's mother and bring up that crucial point. It was going to be beautiful — a real shocker!

"The day of the trial arrived, February fourteenth — Valentine's Day.

"The Small Claims Court judge urged us to try to settle the case. After a confab with my opponent, I reluctantly informed the court that, in honor of Valentine's Day, we had settled the case. The judge laughed and dismissed the action."

That's the way if often goes with lawsuits, large or small. You can't wait to introduce that devastating piece of evidence, or present that block-buster argument, or both, and then your perceived "moment of glory" is snatched away by a last-minute settlement of the case. But, hey, the glorification of the lawyer ain't the point of the exercise. Litigation can be horribly hard on the wallet, and the nerves, and so it's always better to settle if you can.

A civil case doesn't have to involve billions to attract a lot of attention. Why, a teeny-weeny lawsuit recently made a big stir internationally. It also proved the truth of William Congreve's famous observation:

> Heaven has no rage like love to hatred turned,
> Nor hell a fury like a woman scorned.

In May 1989, people all around the world were startled beyond description when they read this short, snappy dispatch:

WEST PALM BEACH, Fla. (AP) —
A 15-year-old girl who says she was stood up on prom night wants to get even: She's suing her date for $49.53 for her shoes, flowers and hair-do he never got to see.

Marlon Shadd, a 17-year-old school basketball star, said he called off the date with Tomontra Mangrum a week before the dance. He said he had a good excuse — a broken ankle.

In my column in the Canadian Bar Association's monthly newspaper, *National*, I asked my anxious readers:

"So what do you think? Will Marlon and Tomontra kiss and make up, or will this high-octane addition to the 'litigation explosion' blast its way into court? Will Marlon hobble back into Tomontra's heart, or will her lawyer slam-dunk him into submission? Will the whole sordid story come out in court and, if so, with what cataclysmic results?

"Stay tuned for the electrifying answers to these exciting questions," I added. "I'm going to probe into this momentous case and as soon as I have the scoop I'll flash the word to you."

Well, let me tell you, that Tomontra has one terrible swift sword, for, faster than you can say Melvin Belli, her ex-date coughed up the dough. All of it, costs included.

Marlon's tab totaled $81.28, consisting of Tomontra's pre-prom outlay of $49.53, plus $19.50 she forked over to file her claim in Small Claims Court and $12.25 she dished up to have it served on the dazed defendant.

The defendant repeated that he had good reason for skipping the prom — his broken ankle — and he pointed out that he'd given Tomontra a week's notice to scare up another date. But, no, she had to scare up a lawsuit instead.

"It's stupid," he declared. "She's just freaking out. I don't know what's wrong with her."

At a news conference, called by her, Tomontra said she was trying to prove that young people have to be taken seriously — *that*'s what was "wrong" with her.

"The payment proves that this was not silly at all," she told reporters. "I did what I had to do, and I'm proud of it."

Marlon said he tossed in the towel because he didn't want the case to drag on and on. He'd already learned that sometimes discretion really is the better part of valor.

Clear across Canada, the vast majority of people who sue and defend in Small Claims Court are not represented by lawyers. Not only is it a great deal faster and less expensive than higher tribunals, it's also much more informal and, in effect, encourages litigants to conduct their own cases in court.

But, back in the 1960s and '70s, there was one judge who was dead against do-it-yourself litigation — and she made this extremely clear every time she opened court. I refer to Judge Edra Sanders Ferguson, a former practicing lawyer who presided in Small Claims Court in Toronto from 1962 to 1977. To a generation of law students and lawyers who cut their forensic teeth in her court, she was known simply and affectionately as "Ma" or "Mother" Ferguson.

Her Honor believed strongly in the truth of the old adage: "He who represents himself in court has a fool for a client."

"'Ma' Ferguson was the greatest asset the legal profession ever had in Toronto," says a lawyer who appeared before her many times in his younger days. "There should have been an admission charge for those who wanted to see and hear her open court.

"She'd walk into court in her judicial robes and then sit down and address the audience as follows: 'Let me ask you something. How many people here don't have a lawyer?' About 80 percent of the parties would raise their hands.

"'Now, listen,' she'd say, 'if you were walking along College Street and you got a pain in your chest, would you walk into Toronto General Hospital, go to an operating room, pick up a knife, cut yourself open and operate on yourself? Well, of course not — because *you'd die*!

"'No, you wouldn't operate on yourself, but most of you *would* do something else that makes about as much sense as that — you'd walk into a court of law without a lawyer! I'll give you one last chance. Whoever wants to get a lawyer — go now! I'll adjourn your cases so you can be represented by counsel at the next court.'

"'Ma' would scare the hell out of those do-it-yourselfers. She'd end up with only a few cases to be tried that day because everyone else would be out looking for a lawyer."

Judge Ferguson was widely regarded as a "character" — and as a hard-working, wise and fair adjudicator. Her court was often called a "no nonsense" court and the product thereof was sometimes referred to as "down-home justice."

Her Honor believed strongly that a bit of good old-fashioned "visual evidence" helped tremendously in getting to the heart of matters. She welcomed such evidence whenever it was proffered and, indeed, she carried some of it around with her in her purse.

"'Ma' always had a couple of miniature toy cars in her purse, one red and the other green," says a Toronto lawyer who prefers to remain anonymous.

"Whenever she was trying a case about cars that collided in an intersection, she'd draw the intersection, nice and big, on a legal-size piece of paper, and then she'd say 'Just a minute!' and she'd lean over and rummage through her purse and pull out the toy cars. Then she'd move the cars around on the paper, in accordance with the evidence that was being given, and it helped her to conclude what probably happened when the *real* cars met at the *real* intersection. I've never heard of any other judge doing that. 'Ma' found it extremely helpful. What the hell — different strokes for different folks."

I told quite a few lawyers I was writing about Judge Ferguson and every one of them, as soon as they heard her name, started speaking affectionately about "Ma" — or "Mother" — and her little toy cars.

Judge Ferguson's penchant for visual evidence carried forward into other fields, too, producing plenty more "down-home justice" that folks can't forget. And some of that justice was swift — mighty swift.

In a memorable case heard in the Polish Hall in west-end Toronto, a tailor sued a customer who wouldn't pay for a pair of pants because, he said, they were "too tight in the crotch."

Judge Ferguson sat at a table on the stage, with a theatrical curtain serving as a backdrop.

"Let's see the pants," she said, and the plaintiff handed them up to her.

"Here," she said to the defendant, "go behind the curtain and put these on. I want to see what they look like on you."

"The curtain didn't go all the way down to the stage," a lawyer recalled recently. "You could see the man's pants drop around his ankles and you could see his hairy legs moving up and down as he got into the pants the tailor had made.

"When the fellow came out through the curtain, 'Mother'

walked over to him, glanced at his crotch and announced, 'Judgment for the plaintiff!'"

In another case, a dry-cleaner sued a woman for not paying her bill. The woman brought some drapes in to be cleaned, and she conceded that they were, in fact, cleaned. But she said that they'd also been burned somewhat in the process.

"Where are the drapes?" asked the judge.

"Here they are, Your Honor," said the defendant.

"Ma" Ferguson whipped out the drapes at arms' length, quickly saw what the customer was complaining about, and declared, "Judgment for the defendant!"

"Ma" Ferguson — eighty-three years young at this writing — did a bit of reminiscing in a conversation I had with her recently. When you've dealt with thousands of cases, as she did during fifteen years on the bench, it's hard to know where to start when you're asked to tell about some of the offbeat ones.

One of her recollections concerned a wig-maker who was sued by a dissatisfied customer. The plaintiff said that his rug didn't fit, and he wanted his money back.

"I could tell at a glance that the wig was about ten sizes too small," she told me. "The defendant said, 'Your Honor, something's *happened* to the wig. It was much bigger — and a different color — when I delivered it to the customer.'"

"Ma" Ferguson soon got to the bottom, or the top, of the problem.

"I questioned the plaintiff and learned that he'd put a lot of Vaseline on the wig," she said, "and when he couldn't get the guk off he boiled the wig in washing soda. That made the wig greasy, so for some reason he then put loads of vinegar on it. All that did was change the color of the wig. The man then took a shower with the wig on and, while it was still wet, he combed in colored ink.

"Needless to say, I dismissed the action."

Yes, indeed, things are sure different in the free-wheeling, rough-and-tumble Small Claims Court. Mr. Justice Allan H. Wachowich of Edmonton throws some interesting light on the subject:

"On a Wednesday afternoon, I sat as a Justice of the Court of

Queen's Bench of Alberta on applications involving the Canadian Commercial Bank liquidation, wherein there were nineteen lawyers officially on the record and at least a dozen more observing, and I heard arguments pertaining to $276 million worth of assets in an hour and fifteen minutes.

"The next morning I returned to reality when I was handling a Small Claims Court appeal. The dispute involved two bitter parties and $500 — and it took three and a half hours to dispose of the appeal.

"In the $276 million application, everybody seemed happy. In the $500 matter, neither party seemed happy. At one point, in fact, one of them yelled at me, 'What do you mean?' I replied to that outburst, 'You're deprived of all costs and if you don't apologize you'll be deprived of your judgment!' He apologized.

"For $500 you get abuse. For $276 million you get smiles."

That was downright tame compared with what happened one morning in the 1950s in a Small Claims Court in Toronto.

A certain judge who didn't like making decisions thought he saw a way to significantly reduce the heavy workload he faced that day. It was highly unorthodox, this brain-wave he'd just had, but he thought he'd give it a shot.

As soon as court opened at 10:00 A.M. His Honor announced:

"I want all plaintiffs and their lawyers, if they have lawyers, to go to the right-hand side of the courtroom. All defendants, and all lawyers representing defendants, please go to the other side of the courtroom."

Everyone wondered what the hell this was all about. Then the judge continued:

"I'm going to adjourn court for fifteen minutes. During that time I urge you people to get together and settle your cases. I hope they'll all be settled by the time I come back."

His Honor then officially suspended proceedings for a quarter hour and went backstage for a coffee.

Ten minutes later there was a tremendous commotion and when the judge and others peeked into the courtroom they must have thought they were watching "Hockey Night in Canada."

Many of the parties were shouting at each other and more than a few had lapsed into fisticuffs.

Police were called in to tame the unruly mob and as he reconvened court the judge was resigned to the fact that he'd just have to do things the hard way.

David H. Jack, Q.C., of Fergus, Ontario, has a story that illustrates the informality of Small Claims Court — at least the one where he serves as a part-time judge.

A decade or so ago, a new clerk of Dave's court was sworn into office. He was a friendly, cheerful fellow who knew a thing or two about how to open court, but damn little about how to close it.

"The first day he was on the job," Dave recalls, "the clerk proclaimed: 'Hear ye, hear ye, the Eighth Division Court of the County of Wellington is now in session, Deputy Judge David H. Jack presiding. God save the Queen!'

"When court was over I said, 'Now, Mr. Clerk, we've disposed of all the cases. Please close the court.'

"The clerk had forgotten what he'd been instructed to say in that situation, but he still did a fine job. He looked out at the audience and announced: 'That's all folks! You can go home now!'"

Lawyer David N. Muise of Sydney, Nova Scotia, recalls a case in which courtroom informality was stretched quite a bit farther than it really ought to go.

Muise acted for a Sydney man who sued a carpet dealer in Small Claims Court. The plaintiff alleged that the carpeting he bought for his living room was defective and he said he wanted new carpeting or his money back.

The defendant said that the high-traffic area in front of the TV set took a beating, what with the plaintiff's teenagers sitting on the floor to watch the tube. *That's* what caused the material to wear out prematurely, he told the court.

When he heard this, the plaintiff jumped up and said: "Do you think I'm too fuckin' poor to have fuckin' chairs? My fuckin' kids don't sit on the fuckin' floor! They're not a bunch of fuckin' animals!"

The plaintiff was severly chastised by the court for his intemperate language and he apologized profusely, as follows:

"Sometimes when I get fuckin' excited I can't control my fuckin' language! I'm awful fuckin' sorry!"

The silver-tongued orator's lawyer, David Muise, remarks: "I didn't speak at that time because I was laughing too hard."

Lindsay, Ontario, lawyer Donald J. Warner, Q.C., loves to tell a tale that was told to him by one of his law professors, Bora Laskin, long before Laskin became Chief Justice of the Supreme Court of Canada.

Back in the 1930s, law student Laskin did a prodigious amount of preparation for his first-ever trial in Division Court, the tribunal that's now called Small Claims Court.

In researching the law, Laskin was thrilled to discover a previous court decision that he was sure would turn him into a winner. The precedent was smack-dab on point and, what's more, it was a decision of the Supreme Court of Canada — the highest court in the land. Since Division Court was the nation's *lowest* civil court, the judge was obliged to follow the "clincher" case that Laskin had unearthed in the library.

But that's not how things went. The judge cared not a fig for the decision of the highest court and found against Laskin's client.

"I don't understand, Your Honor," said the losing counsel. "I told you about the decision of the Supreme Court of Canada and you have totally ignored it. How can this be?"

"This is *my* court, young fellow!" snapped the judge.

"Yes, but — "

"Do you plan to appeal my decision, sonny?" asked the judge.

"Well, as you know, Your Honor, I can't," Sonny Laskin replied. "To be permitted to appeal, my client would have to have a claim of at least $100. He's claiming only $76.41."

"That's right," said the judge, "and that's also why I say the hell with the Supreme Court of Canada!"

In Toronto, generations of admiring lawyers and law students appeared before Judge Frederick Montye Morson, a wise and witty jurist who must have heard more small-claims cases than anyone else in history.

Morson was appointed to the County Court of the County of

York on June 4, 1891 — the last official act of Prime Minister Sir John A. Macdonald — and he served on that court until his retirement at the age of eighty-two, in 1934. For the first thirty-nine of those forty-two years, "Monty," as he was affectionately called, also presided in Division Court, a branch of the County Court that arbitrated small-claims disputes. When a reporter asked him how many such cases he'd disposed of, "Monty" Morson answered, "at least 250,000."

A 1913 article in *Star Weekly* magazine gave this vivid description of Judge Morson in action:

"No judge or lawyer from the United States thinks his visit to Toronto is complete without a visit to the Division Court, if it is in session. There, in the seclusion of a back seat, or in a place of honour on the bench, he sits agape at the way in which all records are broken in the administration of justice, and yet unerringly each receives his due. Then, when he returns to his own country, the first meeting of the state law association, or the first issue of his favorite legal magazine, contains his appreciation of the way he saw legal issues disposed of by 'a real judge' when he was up in Canada. But dignity is never sacrificed for speed, nor does a litigant leave the court rankling under a sense of injustice because he believes that he has not been given opportunity to present his case fairly."

Judge Morson preferred common sense to long arguments. The latter made him edgy and impatient.

A young lawyer once appeared in Division Court with a dozen or more legal tomes lined up on the counsel table and Morson snapped, "What are those for?"

"These books contain the law in respect of my case," said counsel, and His Honor replied, "Well, just watch me change it!"

"Monty" always called the shots the way he saw them. At one trial, a lengthy parade of witnesses testified on behalf of the plaintiff, but only two or three supported the cause of the defendant.

When the evidence had all been presented, Judge Morson turned to the defense lawyer and said, "There's a lot of evidence against you."

"Numerically, they have the advantage," the lawyer conceded.

"Well," replied Morson, "I'm going to give a numerical judgment."

William M. Carlyle, Q.C., of Vancouver will never forget a couple of problems he experienced in Small Claims Court in the late 1940s. The first problem was that the man on the bench had absolutely no legal training. The second problem was that the man on the bench seemed to think that cars were really dogs, and, presumably, vice versa.

Take it away, Bill:

"I was a student at the time, appearing for a plaintiff who was suing for damage done to his car by the defendant's car. I was confident that I had a winning case until the magistrate, a lay person, pronounced the following decision immediately upon hearing the defendant testify that this was the first accident that his car had been involved in:

"'In keeping with the adage that every dog is entitled to its first bite, it is my decision that the defendant's car is entitled to its first accident. Case dismissed.'"

David Acri, an articling law student in London, Ontario, recalls the problems he had with a pushy witness in his courtroom debut:

"Two years ago I was working in my father's law firm in Brampton. While I had been to court many times to watch my father, I had never conducted a trial myself.

"My father had provided some advice regarding a 'slip and fall' claim an out-of-province visitor had against the Brampton Public Works Department. After a strong letter and a few phone calls, the matter was settled quietly and amicably.

"The trouble arose when my father submitted a bill for his services. Some time later, he received a letter from his client with a cheque for one dollar 'for services *not* rendered.' It's one thing not to pay a bill; it's even worse to offend someone that way.

"The matter ended up in Small Claims Court. I was to be 'counsel' and my father was my 'star witness.' I soon learned that after twenty-plus years in practice my father knew full well that

Small Claims Court isn't anything like a big murder trial on the Perry Mason show.

"I was still making my opening remarks when, glancing up from my notes, I saw my father up on the stand, having himself sworn in! He waited, somewhat impatiently, until I was ready to proceed. I managed to get in one question, 'Do you recall the facts in the case at bar?' when Dad completely took over the proceedings.

"When he concluded his story, I meekly stated that I had no further questions and sat by as he was cross-examined by the former client. I was confused and embarrassed and I found myself wondering when Perry Mason would have stood up and objected.

"In the end, we won. The judge agreed with my father that there should be some remuneration for the time spent and skill employed in helping the client.

"Since then, I've gone to court on many occasions, often successfully, but never since have I had as much trouble as I did with the 'star witness' in my very first case."

Colin D. McKinnon, Q.C., of Ottawa has a memorable tale about problems presented by an out-of-province, out-of-country lawyer who some suspected might also be out of his mind. It's an inspiring story of the eventual triumph of justice, and it goes like this:

Back in the 1950s, a noted U.S. trial attorney, now deceased, was the guest speaker at the annual dinner of the Carlton County Bar Association, held at the posh Royal Ottawa Golf Club.

"The speaker," says McKinnon, "was an egomaniac who went on and on about his fantastic law practice and his endless string of stupendous courtroom victories — multi-million-dollar case after multi-million-dollar case. To use an old cliché, the natives were restless. It wasn't long before half the audience was fed up with him, and by the time he finished most of the others felt that way, too."

Rising to his feet to thank the guest speaker was Lionel Choquette, Q.C., a distinguished lawyer and renowned orator who later was appointed to the Canadian Senate.

"Well," he began, in his warm, Gallic manner, "it's been a wonderful experience to hear such stories about these multi-million-dollar actions and, I must say, I'm very, very impressed with these stories. And, you know, we, too, in the Ottawa Valley, have cases that are important. Why, only today, in the village of L'Orignal, I took over a trial in the Division Court for my good friend and distinguished counsel Lorenzo Lafleur, Q.C., who was unavoidably detained in another Division Court."

The hot-shot attorney was starting to seethe.

"It was a very interesting case, with many fascinating problems," Choquette told his chuckling colleagues. "It had to do with the sale of a horse for $185. You know, we argued all day on that case and I had to hurry to get here in time for this dinner. I haven't had an opportunity yet to give a report on the case to my good friend, Lorenzo Lafleur."

While the guest speaker glowered and fumed, Choquette continued.

"Oh," he exclaimed, "I just saw Lorenzo in the audience! Lorenzo, you know that case you sent me?"

"The one about the horse?" shouted Lorenzo.

"Yes, the one about the horse."

"How did it turn out?"

"I'm sorry, Lorenzo, I really am, but I *lost*!"

Then, turning to the famous guest speaker, Choquette said, "Thank you so much for coming here tonight, sir, and telling us about *your* cases."

The audience rose and wildly applauded the man who thanked the speaker.

9

WRONG MISTAKES

WE MADE TOO MANY WRONG MISTAKES.

Yogi Berra

BAD SPELLERS OF THE WORLD, UNTIE!

anonymous graffito

Look, we all have days when our line score reads: "No runs, no hits, twelve errors." After all, no one's perfect. As that great philospher, Archie Bunker, once observed: "God don't make no mistakes. That's how He got to be God."

From time to time, in everyone's life, a few boners, bloopers, or boo-boos are bound to crop up — but they sure ain't welcome.

And no one likes to take the rap for a blunder, either. Franklin P. Jones said it perfectly: "Honest criticism is hard to take — particularly from a relative, a friend, an acquaintance, or a stranger."

But, hey, it's not all gloom and doom. Flubs and foul-ups can be fun — at least for the other guy. Some gaffes are great, some miscues marvelous. Clinkers can cause you to chuckle and typos can trigger a titter or two.

The legal world provides all of these kinds of stimulation — and then some. Tarry a while and I'll show you what I mean.

Sean Kelly, a lawyer in Bracebridge, Ontario, leads off with this dispatch:

"My clients, a Jewish doctor and his wife from Toronto, were involved in a bitter dispute with a neighbor concerning an extremely large cottage constructed by the neighbor. The building substantially obstructed the view that the doctor and his wife had from their cottage.

"I engaged the services of an independent appraiser to comment on the possible devaluation of the property owned by the doctor and his wife. The appraiser's report included the following: 'The subject property is spacious and well-treed and has a gentile slope towards the water.'"

As language experts will attest, "typo-itis" is a highly contagious disease. Around the same time I received the foregoing, Provincial Court Judge Pat Curran wrote from Halifax to advise that the pre-sentence report in a recent indecent exposure case stated: "Between January 31, 1988, and June 25, 1989, the accused exposed his gentile organs in the presence of . . ."

Crown Counsel Steve Stirling, of Port Alberni, British Columbia, submitted this snippet from a pre-sentence report: "It would certainly appear that the accused has roots in the community, as he has been in the excavating business for himself for the last two years."

And, for good measure, Steve tossed in an excerpt from a report prepared by a police officer: "April 23, 1980 — observed subject sit stationary at 3rd Avenue and Angus at a high rate of speed."

Judge Dwayne W. Rowe of the Federal Court of Canada tells of a bestiality case that was heard in Newfoundland:

"It was alleged that the accused had intercourse with a horse," His Honor says, "and the first sentence of the pre-sentence report read, 'The accused comes from a stable background.'"

One day in late 1989 the Kamloops (British Columbia) *Daily News* reported: "Three-month suspended sentences handed to

102 anti-abortionists in Vancouver are 'a mis-carriage of justice,' the vice-president of the local Pro-Life Society said on Monday."

Edmonton lawyer Peggy J. Blair recalls a case in which she prosecuted a man who was charged with sexual assault. The evidence disclosed that the fellow had a strong leaning towards oral sex.

Defense counsel introduced into evidence a letter from the accused's employers. It said that the accused was "extremely well-licked" by the people he worked with.

In Newfoundland, "denominational education" is a hot issue: should the government keep paying for schools that are affiliated with religious denominations? Note the word *affiliated.*

St. John's lawyer William H. Goodridge sent me part of a legal brief that could give the impression that matters have deteriorated, indeed. It reads: "It is clear that the Education Act of 1927 enshrined the principle of denominationally-afflicted school board membership, a principle that survived Confederation. The principle of denominationally-afflicted school board membership subsists ... "

What the hell's going on in the dairy industry? An Alberta court reporter was startled to discover this sentence in the transcript of a witness' testimony: "They were going to transfer title to him of $500,000 worth of their brewed cows."

Another court reporter bumped into this blooper in a transcript: "Did the dysentery leave you in a weekend condition?"

The Alberta court reporter who perpetrated this paragraph was probably "in a weekend condition" at the time:

"One of the transient settlers came up and said to me, 'You shouldn't hire those people because they are religious phonetics.' I knew they were religious phonetics because I myself have been described as a religious phonetic, having found another way to God. I believe in religious phonetics, so I automatically resent it when people class other people as religious phonetics."

Some judges sure know how to lay down the law. Edmonton court reporter Christie Stone came across this judicial outburst in a transcript:

THE COURT: This is the kind of reprehensible conduct that can't be condomed, and will not be condomed.

I always thought convicts got paid something while in prison, even if it was only "peanuts." But another Edmonton court reporter, Alberta Unger, showed me I was wrong. She discovered this in a transcript:

THE COURT: As required by the Criminal Code, I sentence you to imprisonment for life without eligibility for payroll until you have served twenty-five years of your sentence.

And pipe this one:

Q. Did you have any record of this transaction?
A. Well, I had some hand-knitten rotes.

In *More Court Jesters*, I revealed some of the "dictation gems" of an overworked Ontario lawyer, said specimens having been preserved by his secretary and presented to him when he went on the bench. I received these atrocities from the perpetrator himself (what a sport!) and, though he didn't ask me to, I refrained from naming him. I extend him the same courtesy again, now that he's making a return engagement.

   Yes, by popular demand, the Unknown Jurist returns to tell more of his sordid sins, which are as follows:

- "Write to Mrs. Smith . . . Dear Mr. Smith."
- "There are two listings in the phone book for this man, but one of them is unlisted."
- "Craig is an eighteen-year-old male boy."
- "We must note the location of the five-foot-deep holes to be dug, as they will be returned to you upon completion of the digging."

- (In a will): "I direct my trustees to provide a good Christian burial by myself . . ."
- (In another will): "To pay the proceeds of any insurance policy to my brother Steve, on the condition that I be alive at the time of my death."
- "This transaction closed on the 3rd of Jane, 1975."
- "Interest is payable half-yearly on the 30th day of April and the 30th day of October of each month."
- "Then do an Argument on behalf of the Repellant."
- "Write a letter on my mother . . ."
- "I then had a discussion with City Hall."
- "The plaintiff, Ann Michal, was the husband of the plaintiff, George Michal."
- "The defendant used to live with his mother, who is now deceased, whereabouts unknown."

The verbal carnage goes on and on, sometimes cropping up in the most unexpected places. Just ask Dennis R. Murray, Q.C., Deputy Solicitor General of British Columbia. One day in 1988, Dennis came across a recipe for "Chocolate Kahlua Balls" in the Victoria *Times-Colonist*. Included in the instructions was the following: "Store in airtight container in cool place with waxed paper between lawyers."

Recently I received a letter from Charles M. Bauer of Ottawa, who served as a court clerk and justice of the peace in St. Boniface, Manitoba, back in the 1950s and '60s. He fondly recalls an entry made by a francophone in the lost-and-found register of the St. Boniface Police Department: "Found: a pair of testicles, gold-rimmed."

Mr. Justice Horace Krever, of the Ontario Court of Appeal, advises: "I had thought that a bond-maid was a thing of the past in these parts. I now have reason to believe that I may have been wrong."

His Lordship referred to an affidavit that was filed in court by a man who was applying for bail pending an appeal. The document read in part as follows: "My surety in the amount of $100,000 was my stepfather, who put up my mother and his home in order to qualify."

Retired Toronto lawyer Thomas F. C. Cole tells of a couple of boo-boos commited by "temporary typists" who apparently knew damn little about amending bylaws and meats and cheeses. The first specimen states: "The shareholders will be asked to confirm an unending bylaw." The other declares: "After the meeting, the members discussed various leets and Jesus."

Calgary lawyer Fred L. Scott chuckles when he recalls a separation agreement that obliged the husband to pay a stated amount to his wife each month "so long as she shall remain single and shall remain chased."

The word *executor* baffles a lot of folks.

"Homedrawn wills always provide legal practitioners with plenty of headaches, as well as the odd bit of laughter," writes J. A. Sissons, a lawyer in Niagara Falls. "A client of our firm, in writing out his own will, intended to state that my partner, J. R. Boyce, was to be executor. But he wrote: "Attorney J. R. Boyce of law firm of Martin & Sheppard to be executed after all expense pd.'"

A party who has expired is known as "the deceased," right? In most quarters, yes. But according to zillions of estate forms recently distributed by a certain trust company — a sample of which was sent to me by Toronto lawyer Clifford S. Goldfarb — it appears that, miracle of miracles, the dearly departed hasn't departed at all. He must have lost weight, though, for the forms refer to him as "the decreased."

Yes, siree, "typo-itis" abounds. Recently, I received a letter from a lawyer, enclosing a dandy typo. The very first words of the letter were: "On the topic of typographical erros ..."

After settling a case, Hamilton lawyer Robert A. Otto received a letter from his opponent which said in part: "Please provide the settlement proceeds and the release documentation which you wish our client to sing."

In an article pertaining to proposals for new laws to govern the legal profession in British Columbia, a lawyer's newspaper noted: "The proposals also would give the competency committee a strong mandate to set standards of competence and provide the discipline committee with power to disbar a lawyer for competence when . . ."

A document filed a few years ago in the Supreme Court of Nova Scotia described a certain Youth Court Judge as "the Tough Court Judge." And, according to a newsletter that fell into my hands, the Durham Region Law Association, in Ontario, recently chose an extremely inappropriate way to reward its president for his loyalty and leadership. They gave the poor fellow a "plague."

When it comes to goof-ups, though, it's hard to top the chap you're about to meet.

In 1988, a Toronto man who had forty-four previous convictions, many of them for robbery, was found guilty of bank robbery. The note he handed to the teller was short and (like its author) punchy: "This is a up."

The judge sent him up — the river, that is — for three years.

Slips of the tongue can be great fun, too, and what better place to find them than the courtroom? With all that talking going on, it's just a matter of time before somebody blurts out some damn-fool thing.

In a recent impaired-driving case in Halifax the Crown Attorney told the court: "The accused was driving the car erotically down the road."

Judges are human too, you know, and so they're bound to commit the occasional boo-boo. One judge asked a defendant who'd just been arraigned: "How do you plead to the charge, Mr. Guilty?"

Another jurist, trying his first criminal case, was *ever* so careful to avoid making an error that could lead to the ordering of a new trial. For three days he was perfection itself and, with mere moments left before his duty was discharged, he said to the jury, "Now, ladies and gentlemen, when you retire to the Guilty Room . . ."

A judge trying a bigamy case informed a witness who claimed that in Nigeria a man could have as many wives as he wanted, "In this country we only have monotony."

Erin, Ontario, probation officer James Schaffter recalls a case in which a man was charged with contributing to juvenile delinquency. The judge told the accused he should be ashamed of himself for "contributing to this young person's sexual immortality."

Vernon, British Columbia, court reporter Bernard Loomis captured these slips of the tongue:

* "I understand that two of your children are married to each other at this point."
* "I found him to be very open, straightforward, very sincere and apparently very conscious."
* *Q.* And the children are living at home with your wife? *A.* Yes, they're living at home with the kids.

London, Ontario, court reporter Ellen Vezina sends this "slippo" for your consideration:

COUNSEL: If you'll forgive me for saying so, Your Honor, it's as plain as the nose on my face.

Toronto lawyer Martha Binks was a bit flustered at a recent examination for discovery. She had two well-prepared opponents to contend with and, because of the temporary absence of the person who usually swore in witnesses, she had to attend to this chore herself.

Martha says she has absolutely no idea why she instructed the witness as follows: "Please take the bottle in your right hand."

Near the end of a frustrating day in court, in which his opponent had given him a very rough ride indeed, a lawyer began his final argument thusly: "As Your Honor can see by all the evidence that's been prevented today . . ."

At a probate hearing, an American lawyer, speaking of his deceased client, told the presiding judge: "I knew William A. Larsen in his lifetime and for many years prior thereto."

Lt. Col. D. Brian Murphy, of Ottawa, supplied me with a partial transcript of a Canadian military trial. A snippet thereof reads as follows:

Q. What position was he in while he was being searched?
A. He had two hands on the wall, sir, and two on the ground.

Provincial Court Judge Pat Curran, of Halifax, sends this tidbit from a recent impaired driving case:

Q. Officer, why did you give the accused a breathalyzer demand?
A. Because of his condition and my experience as a person under the influence of alcohol.

London, Ontario, court reporter Gail McGilvray skewered this specimen:

Q. I understand you were at the dentist today and you may have some problem communicating.
A. If I sound a little thick-tongued, it is because I just had a filling in my tongue.

Crown Counsel Steve Stirling, of Port Alberni, British Columbia, recently prosecuted a man who'd been sniffing cocaine regularly. Steve advises that the defense counsel, when making a "pitch" on behalf of his client, said to the judge: "He is going to have to keep his nose clean, realizing that he is going to blow it if he gets into any more trouble."

Sault Ste. Marie, Ontario, lawyer R. Jack Falkins reports on a recent court case: "A local lawyer, in the heat of a contested custody motion, was trying to gain custody for her client, the wife, by complaining of the husband's alleged use of steroids. While recounting the wife's various allegations, counsel told the court that her client 'entered the home one day and found a cache of hypodermic noodles.'"

Jack added this brief note: "They picked me up off the floor."

Rodney E. Follwell, a lawyer in Belleville, Ontario, sends this communiqué:

"Recently I was involved in a trial with a number of other counsel. It was a matter regarding an application by the Children's Aid Society to make a child, whom I was representing, a Crown ward.

"On the eve of the trial date, which had been set for weeks, the parents, who I'm sure knew that their chances of success were very slim, discharged their counsel and engaged the services of a new one. New counsel attended at the time set for trial and requested an adjournment.

"The matter had been dragging on and on and I vigorously opposed any adjournment. Of course, the trial judge was going to have the adjournment, and he did, stating, however, that he would not consider any more applications for adjournment unless there was 'a serious death.'"

And that reminds me . . .

One day, back in the 1940s, a Vancouver lawyer, seeking an adjournment of a trial on health grounds, was trying to impress Judge C. J. Lennox with just how ill his client was.

"Your Honor," he said, "the deceased is a sick man."

10

Linguistic Mayhem

I'VE BEEN LAID UP WITH THE INTENTIONAL FLU.

Samuel Goldwyn

Movie mogul Goldwyn could moider da mudder tongue pretty good. He's the fellow who said "Include me out" and "This makes me so sore it gets my dandruff up." He's also the author of "If I could drop dead right now, I'd be the happiest man alive!" and, of course, the ever-popular "A verbal contract isn't worth the paper it's written on."

And, while on the subject of verbal carnage, one mustn't forget, even momentarily, that legendary linguist and grammarian, Jimmy Durante. "The Schnozz" admitted that he got "a little neuralgic" for the old days, and when asked what kind of books he preferred he said he read mostly "non-friction."

Now there's no denying that Sam and Jimmy could mangle and mutilate with the best of them, but, in my humble opinion, the wreckage they left in their wake doesn't quite stack up to the debris that was dumped by former Toronto mayor Allan ("Lampy") Lamport, whose credits read in part as follows: "If I'm going to be pushed off a cliff, I want to be there;" "You can lead a dead horse to water but you can't make him drink;" "It has all the earmarks of an eyesore;" "We've got to act wisely or otherwisely;" "I deny the allegations and I deny the allegators;" "It's like pushing a car uphill with a rope;" "Bring my friends a variety of assorted sandwiches;" and "Let's not discontinue it, let's drop it."

Sam and Jimmy and Lampy would feel right at home in the legal world, where linguistic mayhem is committed on a regular basis. Why, it's downright disgusting what happens there — folks screwing up their syntax, mangling their metaphors, and, yes, even dangling their participles in public.

Words are the raw material of the courts. You can't avoid them, any more than you can avoid the air you breathe. Words, words, words, ricocheting endlessly around the courtroom! Familiar words, unfamiliar words. Big words, little words, and everything in between. It can make your head spin and leave you wondering, "Doesn't anyone ever shut up around here?"

Yes — when court's over. Till then, the talk drones on. And if you're one of the folks who's testifying, it would help a great deal if you knew what the hell the questions mean. For the most part, that depends on understanding the words that are tossed your way.

Sometimes a witness has no idea what a particular word means, but, instead of admitting this and asking for clarification, he or she just forges ahead and hopes for the best. This frequently causes people within earshot to double up with laughter. Other witnesses provoke the same response by butchering various words beyond recognition — just like good old Lampy and Jimmy and Sam.

Let's drop in on some courtrooms and study this matter up close. We'll warm up with a few short snappers:

- •Q. Did you tell your lawyer that your husband had offered you indignities?
  A. He didn't offer me nothing. He just said I could have the furniture and the cat.

- •Q. Were you in the vicinity of the accused when he committed the crime?
  A. No, but I was standing next to him.

- •Q. Were you present at the inception of the altercation?
  A. No, but I was there when the fight started.

•*Q.* Have you had any prior accidents?
 A. No. And I didn't have any before then, either.

•*Q.* Does Mr. Brown frequent that locale with regularity?
 A. What?
 Q. Well, does Jerry hang around the pool hall a lot?

•*Q.* Was he home frequently?
 A. Yeah, when he wasn't away.

•*Q.* What were you charged with?
 A. Drinking while intoxicated.

•*Q.* Do you have any trouble understanding English?
 A. No, I don't got no trouble with the English.

•*Q.* Other than traffic court convictions, have you ever pleaded
  guilty to or been convicted of a felony or misdemeanor?
 A. Mr. Who?
 Q. Misdemeanor.
 A. Who's Mr. Meanor?

•*Q.* What kind of specialist did you say your wife's doctor was?
 A. I think she said he's a vaginacologist.

Crown Counsel Steve Stirling, of Port Alberni, British Columbia,
files this exhibit:

•*Q.* Do you have anything to say before I pass sentence?
 A. Yes, I wasn't intoxnicated.

Greg Currie, of Toronto, recalls a trial in his native Cape Breton
in which a woman testified that the accused took her for a ride
in his car and then became over familiar with her:

•*Q.* Did he have an orgasm?
 A. No, sir, he had a Ford Fairlane.

Niagara Falls lawyer Elijah (Nick) Carter asked a woman, "Do you know whether your husband was born in wedlock?" and she replied, "No, in Owen Sound."

Jill Scrutton, a lawyer in London, Ontario, recalls a stabbing case which featured the following courtroom dialogue:

Q. Now, ma'am, where were these other people in proximity to you?
A. Oh, they were all a little younger than I am.

Sault Ste. Marie, Ontario, lawyer R. Jack Falkins says that one day, several years ago, he asked one of his secretaries to interview a client about his assets in order to complete a financial statement that had to be filed in court. The other secretaries were within earshot, and this is what they heard:
"Do you have any bank accounts?"
"No."
"Do you have any RRSPS?"
"No."
"Do you have any stocks?"
"No."
"Do you have any bonds?"
"No."
"Do you have any debentures?"
"No, my teeth are my own."

In 1986, London, Ontario, court reporter Gail McGilvray caught a witness saying, "I asked them for a ballpark figure because I wanted to be more accurate."

Philippe Desjardins of Ottawa is a retired CBC executive who stays active by attending court regularly. Philippe has been doing this since the early 1980s. He relates that in a recent criminal case the defendant, who wanted to be tried in another community, announced to the court that his lawyer would be applying for "a change of menu."

In another courtroom, Philippe says, a law student who wanted a case remanded asked the judge for "a one-week reprimand for my client."

And (move over, Mr. Berra) Philippe also heard a defense lawyer state: "My client sometimes says things that may be misconstrued the wrong way."

Judge David Kent, who serves on the Provincial Court (Family Division) in Sarnia, Ontario, sends this extract from a transcript:

WITNESS: I told her to destruct counsel.
JUDGE: I'm sorry, what did you say?
WITNESS: I mean detain counsel.

One of Judge Kent's colleagues, Judge F. S. Fisher, who presides in Toronto, sends along this little gem: "A Public Health nurse in Hamilton recently asked a teenage girl whether she was sexually active. The girl replied, 'No, I just lie there.'"

And another confrère, Judge Grant Campbell of the Provincial Court (Family Division) in Kitchener, tells of a case in which the Children's Aid Society asked that a child be taken away from his parents and made a Crown ward. In the witness box, the child's father said: "I don't want you to make any kid of mine a Crown wart."

Provincial Court Judge Pat Curran of Halifax writes: "In a breathalyzer case I heard in October 1989, a witness who was asked what it was that brought the accused to his attention replied, 'It was his eradicate driving.'"

Midland, Ontario, lawyer Douglas G. Haig, Q.C., once represented a man who was arrested, along with many others, when police raided a gambling establishment.
    "I'm in terrible trouble, Mr. Haig," the client said when he retained the lawyer. "I'm a found-out."

David N. Muise, a well-known lawyer in Sydney, Nova Scotia, was consulted recently by a man who was mighty concerned about all the silence he was getting from the Workers' Compensation Board.

"I disappeared before the Board two years ago," he said, "and I haven't heard from them since."

Muise, a raconteur extraordinaire, has many wonderful yarns about colorful Cape Breton characters — including a big, beefy Sydney cop named Hughie R. MacDonald.

One day, back in the 1940s, Hughie R. arrested two men and a woman for being drunk and disorderly in a public place. Moments after they were put in the cells, the woman called out, "Oh, officer, I'll need Kotex in the morning," and Hughie R snarled, "Shut up, you'll have Corn Flakes like the rest of them!"

Maxine Strain, of Lethbridge, Alberta, reports that in her city in 1985 an accused man representing himself in court argued that he should never have been charged with impaired driving because on the night in question he was perfectly willing to submit himself to "a pap test."

Edmonton court reporter Chris Brower sends this specimen:
Q. Mr. Smith, what happened at the scene? Were you taken by the police to the police station, or what happened?
A. No, my brother was taken away for impaired driving, and the officer gave me the celebrity test and I passed . . .

Ottawa lawyer Martha Coady writes: "Articling students quickly become adept at attending court and requesting adjournments. Various excuses are usually pleaded and it seems the request, no matter what the excuse, always begins with, 'My principal is currently . . .' or 'Opposing counsel is currently . . .' or 'My client is currently . . .'

"I guess my fellow articling student became a bit too accustomed to using this phrase. One day, while appearing in Small Claims Court, he requested an adjournment for a trial scheduled to proceed that day.

"Using the all-too-familiar phrase, the student commenced his request by stating that his client was 'currently dead.'

"The judge didn't bat an eye, but merely looked at the student and asked, 'And will your client still be dead next week?'"

A lot of folks get mighty confused by the lingo of the law. Provincial Court Judge G. J. Barnable, of Placentia, Newfoundland, tells us about one of them:

"Every year my court clerk, Geraldine Smith, is asked by the technical school to permit one of its secretarial students to do the in-service training portion of the course in her office. These students spend a week helping out and seeing how the office works. They are often bewildered by the procedures.

"One student was particularly bewildered by the procedure for enforcing the collection of fines by the issuance of warrants where there was a jail term fixed in default. When the warrant had been effected, the police would make a return indicating the same.

"The clerk came on the scene one day to find her student staring at a returned warrant. Horrified, she handed it over with the awed question: 'They didn't do that to him for speeding, did they?'

"Stamped across the warrant was the shocking statement: 'EXECUTED.'"

It's a sin what some people do with their syntax. For example, take a squint at this sentence in a lawyer's brief: "The trial court erred in ordering a medical examination of appellant's penis in his absence."

If strangled syntax gives you the giggles, I have some other documents you should definitely peruse. The first, sent to me by Mr. Justice Perry Meyer of the Superior Court of Quebec, contains statements written by motorists who were asked by police to tell briefly how their accidents came about. Here's a smattering of same:

- "I collided with a stationary truck coming the other way."
- "The guy was all over the road. I had to swerve a number of

times before I hit him."

- "I pulled away from the side of the road, glanced at my mother-in-law, and headed over the embankment."
- "I was sure the old fellow would never make it to the other side of the roadway when I struck him."
- "I had been driving for forty years when I feel asleep at the wheel and had the accident."
- "The gentleman behind me struck me on the backside. He then went to rest in the bush with just his rear end showing."
- "I was on my way to the doctor with rear-end trouble when my universal joint gave way, causing me to have an accident."
- "The telephone pole was approaching. I was attempting to swerve out of its way when it struck my front end."
- "I was thrown from my car as it left the road. I was later found in a ditch by some stray cows."

If you're panting for more of this sort of thing, consider these memos received by the Toronto Welfare Department:

- "Dear Sir: You asked me to forward my marriage certificate and six children. I had seven but one died and was baptized on the half sheet of paper here."
- "This is to let you know that Mrs. Jones has not had any clothes for a year and has been visited by her minister regularly."
- "Please find out if my husband is dead, as the man I am living with won't do anything until he is sure."
- "I am glad to report that my husband who was reported missing is now dead."
- "Please send the money at once. I have fallen into errors with my landlord."
- "I cannot get sick pay. I have six children. Can you tell me why?"
- "I am forwarding my marriage certificate and my three children, one of which was a mistake, as you can see."
- "My husband got his project cut off two weeks ago, and I haven't had any relief since."
- "Unless I get my husband's money soon, I will be forced to lead an immortal life."

- "In accordance with your instructions, I have given birth to twins in the enclosed envelope."
- "I want my money back as quick as I can get it. I have been in bed with the doctor for two weeks and he doesn't do me any good. If things don't improve, I will have to send for another doctor."
- "With reference to your letter regarding dental inquiry — the teeth in the top are all right, but the ones in my bottom are hurting terribly."

Mr. Lewis Carroll put it this way:

> "When I use a word," Humpty Dumpty said in a rather scornful tone, "it means just what I choose it to mean — neither more nor less."
>
> "The question is," said Alice, "whether you can make words mean so many different things."
>
> "The question is," said Humpty Dumpty, "which is to be the master — that's all."

History — and literature — were repeated in a recent court case in Toronto, as seen in the transcript that follows. Toronto lawyer Robert L. Colson, the cross-examiner therein, tells us all the background we need to know:

"The case involved a couple who alleged serious and substantial misrepresentations on the part of a stockbroker, which induced them to buy a penny stock which ultimately proved valueless. The wife's evidence on the meaning of 'a couple' and on the question of whether or not she used the word 'bet' was quite telling."

Apart from a change of name for the witness, here's the verbatim account of what was said:

Q. In terms of your overall investment objectives, which I understand to be that you have a mortgage-free home within two months —

A. Or three.

Q. — that you be able — pardon me?

A. Or three.

Q. Well, you said "two."

A. You said "a couple of months."

Q. No, you said "two."

A. Would you check that, please, because I'd like to clarify it if I said "two." I thought it said "a couple of months."

MR. DAVIS: The word is "couple."

MR. COLSON: In any event, what do you understand "a couple" to be?

A. Well, a few months, less than a year.

Q. You and your husband are a "a couple," aren't you? Less than a year is "a couple" of months in your mind.

A. Well, actually, we — sorry, less than half a year.

Q. Less than half a year is a couple of months?

A. Less than half a year. We had it down in our salary we could almost pay off that mortgage in a couple of months.

Q. Mrs. Watson, you said "a couple of months."

A. Yes, and I'm saying —

Q. Now, are you telling me that a couple of months can be anything under half a year?

A. I used the term "couple" in reference to few, very little, and if that wasn't fair, let me clear it now. I —

Q. How many shoes do you have on your feet, a couple? That's two. Don't you understand that?

A. No, I have a pair of shoes. We don't call shoes "a couple."

Q. Mm-hmm. But we call two "a couple."

A. *You* call two "a couple."

Q. You and your husband —

A. And I'm saying, and I've clarified the context, so had there been any misunderstanding —

Q. No, you're changing your evidence, you're not clarifying the context. You and your husband are "a couple," two. A couple of dollars is *two* dollars.

A. In the way *you* use the term. I'm telling you, I used "couple" differently.

Q. You used "couple" to mean anything under six.

A. I told you the context in which I used the word.

Q. Do you use it to mean anything under six, Mrs. Watson? I suggest to you you don't.

A. If I say "a couple" of cookies, "hand me a couple of cookies," I expect not necessarily two cookies.

Q. Well, how many do you expect, five, six?

A. A handful, how many ever —

Q. A handful, a handful or cookies.

A. Yes, that's the term in which I would have used it.

Q. How many cookies would you expect if you asked for "a few?"

A. The same amount, roughly, whatever a handful is.

Q. Isn't "a few" more than "a couple"?

A. I don't know.

Q. I see. You're a school teacher, you've got an honors degree in English —

A. No, I have a B.A. in English.

Q. You've got a B.A. in English, you have two children, you're thirty-nine years old, you're a sophisticated real estate investor, I suggest to you, and you're —

A. I don't suggest I am sophisticated.

Q. — you're telling me that "a couple" means six or less, or a "handful."

A. Yes.

Q. Is that really your evidence, Mrs. Watson, under oath?

A. Yes.

Q. All right. Well, let's go back, then. Your objective was to have a mortgage-free home in, what, two or three months — or is it two or under six months? You see, you said three —

A. Well, actually, we figured it out that it was around four months. We figured we could have the mortgage-free home with our salary.

Q. So, you don't mean "a couple" of months, you don't mean two or three months, which is what you next said, you don't mean "anything under six months," what you mean is *four* months when you said —

A. I don't know, because we allowed for the fact that there might be other expenses, which is why I was nebulous about how many coming months, because we knew that with our income, that ten thousand, and we're making five thousand a month, we could get cleared up very quickly.

Q. So, then, just so I have it, your evidence now is that you wanted to have a mortgage-free home and your expectation was that you would have that within four months.

A. If nothing unforeseen happened, yes.

Q. And that was your objective —

A. Yes.

Q. — that was what you were working toward.

A. Yes.

Q. And you must have considered, as any reasonable person would, that placing all of your equity in the commodities market would not be consistent with that objective.

A. Very definitely.

Q. And even placing 10 percent of your money in the commodities or the stock market may well turn out to be inconsistent with that objective.

A. I disagree.

Q. Oh. Well, what about 15 percent of your money? Consistent or inconsistent?

A. If we had wanted fifteen, we would have bet — put the fifteen in. I wasn't going to —

Q. Did you say "bet?"

A. No, I didn't.

Q. Oh, you didn't? What did you say, Mrs. Watson? I thought I heard "bet."

A. I started to say that and I stopped because I thought, God, that is the wrong word —

Q. Yes.

A. — and after you do "couple," I thought they're going to —

Q. So you did say it.

A. No, I said I *started* to and I thought, no, that was so wrong.

Q. It wouldn't sound right.

A. Because I said five thousand was what I was prepared to lose, and I knew that was one month's salary and that wouldn't stop my objective.

Q. Mrs. Watson, you're here under oath.

A. I know that, and you can't find very many people as honest as me.

Q. Are you telling me you did not say the word "bet"?

A. I said I started to say it and stopped. That is the truth.

Q. Well, where did you stop? You didn't stop until after you had finished saying it. You are under oath, Mrs. Watson.

A. I know that, and I said I started to say it and I didn't finish it, because it was inaccurate.

Q. Well, what part of it did you say and which part of it that you didn't say?

A. "B-e" and not the "t."

Well, there you have it, folks. Now you know what slippery, treacherous little devils words can be, in or out of court — but especially in. No wonder Sam and Jimmy and Lampy and plenty of others, too, get kind of disoriented when it comes to words.

The plain truth is that words can do you in. The chap who composed the ditty that follows — whoever he was — knew that for sure:

> There was a little lawyer man,
> Who gently smiled as he began
> Her dear husband's will to scan;
> And thinking of his coming fee,
> He said to her quite tenderly,
> "You have a nice fat legacy."
> Next morning as he lay in bed
> With bandages on smashed-in head,
> He wondered what in hell he'd said.

11

MORE STUPID QUESTIONS

Q. I SHOW YOU A PIECE OF COAL, AND I ASK YOU, WHAT IS IT?

A. A PIECE OF COAL.

Q. YES, THAT IS RIGHT.

I assure you that the preceding daffy dialogue actually occurred, in a real trial, not so long ago. What's more, this sort of wackiness has been going on for a very long time. And if we're lucky it will never cease, for in this sad, mad world there are few surer sources of the therapy known as laughter than the good old-fashioned Stupid Question.

A great many folks, I suspect, would heap scorn and ridicule on the perpetrator of the query exhibited above. But not yours truly.

To me, said specimen is a thing of beauty and a joy forever, entitling both author and composition to be enshrined, without further ado, in my internationally renowned Hall of Shame.

That's where truly great Stupid Questions are preserved for posterity. The search for new talent to showcase in that temple of trash virtually never ceases. Yes, hard as it may be to believe, there's always a long line of lawyers storming its portals, begging for admission. Relatively few succeed, and those who do often owe their good fortune to the glowing recommendations of colleagues or court reporters who know a superstar when they hear one.

On this, our third visit to the Hall of Shame, we'll focus on the most recent S.Q.s to be immortalized therein.

We start with the same lawyer who asked the doozie noted above. He's a persistent bloke, always lusting after the limelight, and on only his second try he cracked the Hall again with this beaut: "Where were you when you weren't where you said you were?"

Calgary lawyer J. D. Palmer roped — and successfully sponsored — this worthy S.Q.: "Was it you or your brother that was killed in the war?"

The reply is tops, too: "It must have been my brother. I wasn't in the war."

London, Ontario, court reporter Gail McGilvray, always on the lookout for legal levity, sends this exchange from a 1987 trial in St. Catharines:

Q. What were you doing driving on the road at that time?
A. I was driving my brother home.
Q. Was your brother in the car with you?

In another recent case, Gail bagged this beaut:
Q. What time were you driving on that road?
A. 11:00 P.M.
Q. Was that in the morning?

Then the eagle-eyed Ms. McGilvray snared this lulu:
Q. Just tell me how he was involved in the company. You said not at all. Did you mean not at all?
A. Not at all while I was alive.
Q. You are still alive now?

Shortly after that, Gail, definitely on a roll, garnered this goodie: "Have you ever smelled an odorless solvent before?"

Court reporter Maria Mihailovich, of Hamilton, Ontario, is also a keen chronicler of forensic falderal. Here's a dab of deathless dialogue — with built-in S.Q. — that Maria spotted and preserved for us and future generations:

Q. What is your date of birth?
A. October, 1910.
Q. Do you remember the day?
A. No, but I've been told about it.

In another case, we have this snippet:

Q. Do you remember when Sunday was that week?
A. It followed Saturday.

Ottawa court reporter Doreen Johnson, formerly of Edmonton, recently reeled in a couple of short, snappy S.Q.s:

- A. I guess I was about ten.
  Q. Were you in high school yet?

- A. My legs are very painful.
  Q. Which legs?

Some lawyers must have been issued, not born, for they can't seem to sort out simple relationships within the bosom of a family. Ian Sutherland, a court reporter in Lethbridge, Alberta, preserved this pip for posterity:

Q. And who owned the car?
A. My Mom and Dad.
Q. And they're your parents?

Here's more of the same, from Edmonton court reporter Marie Kennedy, who harpooned this dilly:

Q. I understand, ma'am, that you are the mother of Janice Smith. Is that correct?
A. Yes.
Q. And, as well, you are the mother of Susie Smith?

A. Yes.
Q. And they're sisters?

And, while we're on the subject, get a load of this one:

Q. Mrs. Shahda, is the plaintiff in this case, Michael, your son?
A. Yes, he is.
Q. And I imagine he's been your son all his life, is that correct?

Nanaimo, British Columbia, lawyer John D. Hope has a tasty tale to tell.

"The accused was charged with breaking and entering a high school with intent to commit the offense of theft," John writes.

"The man was caught with a blanket in his arms and a garlic sausage around his neck. The defense was that the accused had no intention of committing a crime; he was merely looking for a place to sleep.

"On cross-examination, defense counsel got a school official to admit that the blanket held by the accused bore no markings or anything else that identified it as the property of the school board.

"Then, carried away with how well he was doing, he asked: 'And have you ever seen *that* garlic sausage before?'"

As I've said before, one shouldn't leap to the conclusion that lawyers who ask such moronic questions as the foregoing are all scatter-brained nincompoops. Actually, in the heat of battle, with so many things swirling around in your noggin, it's pretty easy to pop a Stupid Question. It's easier still if you switch your brain off for a jiffy or think of a question while you're still asking another one. Yes, indeed, the mouth is frequently faster than the mind.

But, let's face it, people love to smirk and guffaw at the damn-fool mistakes of others — it's only human nature, right? They're not going to cease and desist just because I ask them to. So I've decided to plow straight ahead and give 'em what they want — a gaggle of ghastly gaffes.

You should try not to be hard on these folks, though. They're just stumbling along, like the rest of us. Keep saying to yourself,

"There, but for the grace of God, go I." And if that doesn't work — and it rarely does — then, what the hell, you might as well sit back and laugh your evil hearts out.

Misery likes company, they say, and lawyers should be consoled to know that there are also other experienced interrogators who sometimes blurt out Stupid Questions. Sports writers, for example.

Minutes after New York Yankees pitcher Don Larsen threw his historic "perfect game" in the World Series of 1956, a scribe asked him, "Is this the best game you've ever pitched?"

The Toronto *Star* of January 31, 1988, recorded a couple of corkers: "For a lot of people, the high point of Super Bowl week was attained when an earnest young journalist asked Doug Williams of the Washington Redskins how long he'd been a black quarterback. And another reporter hit Dexter Manley with this query: 'If you were a tree, what kind would you be?'"

Fortunately for zillions of folks who require a periodic fix of laughter, Stupid Questions of the court variety can be found in abundance all around the world. For example, consider this recent specimen from Melbourne, Australia: "How far from the chair were you when it hit you?"

And in the spirit of our new free-trade agreement, I present herewith a smorgasbord of S.Q.s from the U.S. of A.:

•*Q.* How many autopsies have you performed on dead people?
 A. All my autopsies have been on dead people.

•*Q.* At the time you first saw Dr. McCarty, had you ever seen him prior to that time?

•*Q.* And have you ever been injured or killed yourself, ma'am?

•*Q.* Do you have any sort of medical disability?
 A. I'm legally blind.
 Q. Does that create substantial problems with your eyesight as far as seeing things?

•*Q.* Now then, Lieutenant, you have investigated many other murders, have you not, where there has been a victim?

•*Q.* Where is Mr. Albert McIntosh now?
 A. He's buried.
 Q. Is he dead now?

•*Q.* And approximately when was that statement made?
 A. About two weeks before she went to the hospital.
 Q. Before her final death?

•*Q.* You say he was cruel to you. What did he do to you?
 A. He hit me and bit me.
 Q. You say he hit you. What did he hit you with?
 A. His fist.
 Q. What did he bite you with?

•*Q.* Did you give your ticket to someone?
 A. Yes.
 Q. And do you remember who that person was?
 A. As I recall, it might have been somebody with a beard.
 Q. Do you remember if it was a man or a woman?

• How long have you practiced surgery as a surgeon?

• Of the types of things you said you were looking for, what types of things do those things that you were looking for relate to insofar as things go?

•*Q.* How were you dressed?
 A. I had on a housedress.
 Q. What material was it made out of, if anything?

•*Q.* Now, officer, on the occasion in question, where were you located, if anywhere?

•*Q.* Would you demonstrate, by standing up, just how he was crouched?

- *Q.* You heard the entire conversation between the lady and the officer?
  A. I can't say I heard every word, no.
  Q. How much of it did you miss?

- *Q.* At any period of time when you lost consciousness, or don't remember what happened, did you see the car change direction or speed?

- *Q.* If the car went up the hill at fifty miles an hour, coming down how far would it have to go before it hit fifty miles an hour? True or false?

- *Q.* Now, Mr. Jones, we don't want you to tell us anything you don't know of your own personal knowledge; not what someone told you, or what you think, but only what you actually know of your own personal knowledge. Now, are you a married man?

Back on the Canadian side of the border, Peter F. Thompson, a lawyer in Midland, Ontario, tells about an assault case he defended when he was a law student in Edmonton. After Peter had examined his client under oath, the Crown Attorney rose to cross-examine him — and her very first question was, "Sir, your father is considerably older than you, I gather?"

Sydney, Nova Scotia, lawyer David N. Muise testified recently in a case in which it was alleged that someone had unlawfully removed equipment from an industrial plant. After much evidence about tell-tale holes that had been found in the building, we have this dialogue:

Q. Isn't it quite obvious, Mr. Muise, that those holes were constructed in the briquette plant to accommodate a certain piece of equipment?
A. I would assume that, I don't know.
Q. And if the equipment were removed from that area, those holes would remain behind, wouldn't they?

A. Yes, they didn't take them with them.

Roger Harris, a Halifax law student, phoned me to report that in a recent trial, across the harbor in Dartmouth, a lawyer asked a witness: "Were you at the house before you got there?"

My faithful correspondent, Philippe Desjardins of Ottawa, heartily agrees with my contention that court is "the best free show in town." He also shares my view that the courtroom is a happy hunting ground for the ever-popular Stupid Question.

In a recent trial, Philippe advises, evidence disclosed that a man wearing nothing but socks jumped to his death from the accused's twelfth-floor apartment.

"I went outside and saw a body in the snow," the wife of the building superintendent told the court. Defence counsel then asked: "Was anybody around?"

And, reporting on a 1984 murder trial in Hull, Quebec, Philippe writes: "After the victim's wife, the star witness in her lover's trial, kept saying 'I don't remember' to most of the questions asked in cross-examination by a veteran defense counsel, the lawyer put a last desperate question to her: 'Would you please tell the court all the things you can't remember?'"

That sort of S.Q. must be highly contagious. Court reporter Gail Debenham sends this specimen from a trial in Edmonton:

Q. That night, when you were at Coreen's house, do you remember everything that happened that night?

A. No, I don't remember it all.

Q. Okay. What part don't you remember about what happened that night?

But enough of this madness! Perhaps, one of these days, I'll open a Hall of Shame for Stupid Answers.

If I do, this will be the first inductee:

Q. Did you have a headache last night?

A. No, sir. The last headache I had was about three or four days ago, and it lasted five days.

12

HANKY-PANKY

THOU SHALT NOT COMMIT ADULTERY.

The sixth commandment

I present herewith a smattering of Canadian court cases pertaining to adultery and various other naughty activities.

Please be aware that these cases, despite their serious subject matter, may cause many persons to chortle, chuckle, giggle, or guffaw. If you have any such reactions, don't try to fight them. Just rejoice in the realization that you're human, after all.

St. John's, Newfoundland, lawyer David C. Day, Q.C., sent me a rip-snorting transcript from one of his recent divorce cases. Before you dive into it, though, I should advise the uninitiated that "rampse" and "rompse" are fine old Newfie words that mean "to fight playfully and noisily; to skylark."

As we look in on the above-mentioned divorce case, the petitioner — let's call her Mrs. Clancy — is on the stand and her lawyer, David Day, is asking her some preliminary questions. Word for word, here's what was said:

Q. I refer next to paragraph six of the petition, Mrs. Clancy, to ask you about your knowledge of your allegation — I summarize in my words — that your incontinent husband consorted with another woman. To begin with, tell His Lordship how you —

A. It wasn't that way at all, Your Honor. It happened right in our marriage bed in Foxtrap. He's the whoremaster. She isn't much better.

Q. Mrs. Clancy, I promise to come to that part of your story in a few questions.

A. No need for any more questions. We'll go to it now.

Q. When did you first suspect your husband was having sexual contact with another woman?

A. When I seen him in my bed with her.

Q. You came into the bedroom unexpected and found your husband and another woman in the sheets?

A. You can say that. Part under, part on the sheets. Anyway, I didn't walk in or nothing. I heard he was rampsing with this one and that one on Friday nights when I go to town [St. John's] to Bingo. Then the rampsing became something more than just rampsing.

HIS LORDSHIP: You know what "rampsing" is, do you, Mr. Day?

MR. DAY: Ramming? No. No. I know the term as "rompsing." Never experienced, at least I don't think so.

HIS LORDSHIP: "Rampsing," also known as "rompsing" in the *Dictionary of Newfoundland English*.

MR. DAY (*resuming his questioning*): Mrs. —

A. Playing around, innocent-like. But what happened later was no innocent matter. She was a real sailor's man. I heard she's contacted everything there is to get.

Q. How did you learn the rampsing became romantic?

A. I hid in the closet one night. I loaned my car to my girlfriend that time so he'd think I was in town. Two o'clock, there's noise downstairs, then on the stairs, then in the bedroom. I came out. Dead on the floor. My husband is alone, a skinful in, being on the beer.

Q. False alarm?

A. Yes, but there was nothing false the next Friday. I didn't go to Bingo that time. I and my girlfriend got in my car and kept a watch. Sure enough, ten o'clock, her and the trooper come to our house, go in, lights on downstairs, then upstairs in the bathroom, back down in the kitchen, back up to the bathroom, then the bedroom, then lights out. And they closed the curtains.

Q. And when the lights went out in your home in Foxtrap that night in June, what, pray tell, what did you do?

A. Plenty.

Q. Let us in on it.

A. Well, we had the plan in place. My friend is a social worker, so you can imagine it was all above board. She had got advice from a lawyer. And we had two tension ladders. And, secret-like, we put the two of them up handy to the bedroom window about 2:00 A.M., when the business is done and all is quiet. But things didn't stay quiet. I got up one ladder. It got stuck first and wouldn't expand up. Anyway, we got them up.

Q. The two ladders?

A. Yes. The social worker up on one and me up the other. Almost fifteen feet off the ground. And I think she had the light. Yes, she had the flashlight. I had the ax. I smashed out the window. The storm window and the inside window and the transit. And ripped down the curtains.

Q. The transom? The wooden bar in the window?

A. Yes. The whole shagging thing. Glass and wood chips and sheers all over the place. The ax got loose from me and hit the bed. And then I shined the light in. No, I mean the social worker shined the light in. And what a sight! I did the looking. The two darlings fast to sleep. Anyway, she shined the light in. The trooper was under the sheets, or at least part under and part on the sheets. He was asleep on his back. About the same time they both sat up and they stared right into the light. My husband and her.

Q. What next happened?

A. I didn't stick around to find out. But I know he went to the Mounties next day and charged me with breaking and entering. But I certainly didn't enter. I only did the breaking. He was the one entering.

Ho-hum, just another day at the courthouse for David C. Day, divorce lawyer.

Day, co-author of a learned textbook on Canadian divorce law, has acted in a great many *un*learned, funny divorce cases — especially the sort that spring from what he calls "the urge to merge."

As demonstrated in my earlier books, *Court Jesters* and *More Court Jesters*, the fact-situations of some of Day's cases appear to have been concocted by Hollywood sitcom writers. In one zany case, for example, a young . . . well, let's get the grisly details from Mr. Day himself:

"Petty Harbor, historically a fishing hamlet and, more recently, also a bedroom community for St. John's twenty-five kilometers away, is noteworthy for its slate-gray seascapes. In 1971, the nocturnal activities of 2 of the 340 married persons then residing there rendered Petty Harbor remarkable for another reason.

"A twenty-eight-year-old cooper [i.e., barrelmaker] suspected his twenty-three-year-old wife of practicing infidelity with a precocious school-boy, who did house-cleaning for the couple, in the bathroom of the couple's bungalow. As a result of the cooper's telephone call to me, I arranged for my partner, David Eaton, to be present for the office consultation.

"In addition to alleging infidelity by his spouse, the cooper charged, during the consultation, that she was sedating him with a derivative of *Cannabis sativa L*, which, he asserted, she shot into his thighs and buttocks by using a pellet gun. In an effort to enhance his credibility, he leaped onto an office chair, dropped his denim overalls and opened the hatch at the rear of his full-body flannel foundation garment, exposing a red polka-dotted posterior.

"On the basis of the information he disclosed and displayed during the consultation, the cooper inquired whether he could found a divorce petition on the ground of adultery or physical cruelty. My advice was that he first furnish me a credible witness or photographs — preferably both. He furnished neither.

"As unfolded in subsequent trial testimony, my client, the principal witness in the case, left my office and purchased a tape recorder and several cassette tapes. He returned to Petty Harbor where he secreted himself in the crawl-space beneath his bungalow and cut a hole through the bathroom floor, behind the cistern, equal to the dimensions of the tape recorder.

"When next he arrived home and discovered his wife already there, and the school-boy's bicycle on the verandah, he got under the bungalow, activated his tape recorder, inserted it into the floor-hole and made an electronic record of whatever was transpiring on the other side of the bathroom floor.

"The tape was not tendered in evidence because, in my opinion, it had recorded only gurgling sounds, equally consistent with the use of various bathroom and human receptacles.

"As it turned out, the tape wasn't required at trial, anyway. The cooper confronted his wife and companion with the tape, in consequence of which their presence together in the bathroom was admitted by them at trial. Thereupon, without permitting any further questions to be asked of them, the judge readily drew inferences of opportunity and inclination, amounting to adultery."

That's the way it goes in cases of alleged hanky-panky. The evidence must convince the court that the suspected sinners had both the inclination and the opportunity to commit adultery — *and* that they took advantage of that opportunity. Inclination without opportunity won't do, and vice versa. In some cases there's plenty of both and yet there's little or nothing to suggest that the suspects succumbed to "the urge to merge." Of course, every case must be decided on its own facts.

Before he went on the bench, Provincial Court Judge C. J. Cannon of Toronto represented a man who sued his wife for divorce when it was discovered that she'd holed up in a motel with a wandering troubadour.

The manageress of the motel testified that the plaintiff's wife and her musical boyfriend spent two weeks at her establishment.

"They hardly ever went out," she said, "and it seemed that the man was always thumping on his guitar. Many guests complained that they couldn't sleep at night and several times I had to ask him to pipe down."

"Two weeks? Two weeks?" remarked the wise and witty Mr. Justice George Walsh. "Madam, he was doing more than playing his guitar!"

District Court Judge Edward J. Houston of Ottawa recalls a divorce case that was tried in the nation's capital:

"The defendant, a dentist, defended the case and testified at trial. When he'd given his evidence, the judge turned to him and said, 'Doctor, the trouble with you is that you've been filling the wrong cavities.'"

Mr. Justice Melvin E. Shannon of the Court of Queen's Bench of Alberta tells about a divorce case he overheard back in his lawyering days.

"Some years ago I was in Divorce Court waiting to present a case," he writes. "The late, legendary Mr. Justice Harold Riley was presiding that afternoon. At that time, adultery was the only basis for a divorce and the evidence of adultery was often provided by private detectives.

"A licenced private detective — a distinguished-looking gentleman with a British accent — was sworn in to give evidence.

"'I was engaged by the plaintiff to obtain evidence of adultery,' he told the court. 'On January 6th, 1960, I followed his wife for some time and saw her enter an apartment building. She proceeded to a suite located on the second floor of the building, which suite was occupied by her lover. I climbed up a tree which provided a vantage point from which I could look into the window and observe what was taking place. I saw the defendant in the suite with her boyfriend and they committed adultery.

"'Don't tell me they committed adultery!' snapped Mr. Justice Riley. 'That is a conclusion for *me* to draw from the evidence. Just give me the facts and *I* will decide whether or not she committed adultery.'

"'Very well, sir, may I refer to my notes?' asked the witness.

"'Yes, of course,' His Lordship replied."

From there on, says Mr. Justice Shannon, the dialogue was as follows:

WITNESS (reading notes): At 8:00 P.M. they were kissing one another. At 8:02 P.M. they were embracing and undressing one another. At 8:04 P.M. they were sinking onto the bed together. (*a long pause and examination of notes*)

HIS LORDSHIP: Yes? Yes?

WITNESS: At 8:06 P.M. I fell out of the tree.

HIS LORDSHIP: Now *that's* adultery! Decree granted.

Judge Dwayne W. Rowe of the Tax Court of Canada reminisces about another Alberta production:

"In a divorce case heard in Peace River, back in the days when adultery was the only ground for divorce, the defendant, a wee slip of a fellow from a nearby village, was given the mandatory warning that he didn't have to admit to adultery unless he wanted to. It was obvious immediately that he couldn't wait to spill the beans.

"He pumped out his chest and proceeded to serialize, one after the other, in great, elaborate fashion, numerous acts of adultery he had committed. Eventually, Mr. Justice Jimmy Cairns, overawed by this carnal confession, said to the defendant, 'I think we've heard enough, sir.'

"'But, My Lord,' the defendant protested, 'my lawyer told me to tell the truth, the whole truth, and nothing but the truth. I'm only up to nine. I've slept with twelve other women, too, and that's just in my village!'

"His Lordship stuck to his guns, however, and then made a classic quip: 'It's very difficult to tell where the evidence ends and the boasting begins.'"

Before major divorce-law reforms were introduced in the late 1960s, anyone seeking a divorce in the Supreme Court of Ontario had to divulge in writing whether he or she had committed adultery in the past and, if so, give certain particulars. This information was put in a sealed envelope, for the judge's eyes only. The general idea behind this now-defunct rule was that you shouldn't squawk to the court about your mate's adultery if you've committed the same sin yourself — unless, of course, you've fessed up to it in that top-secret communiqué.

As a result of that rule, lawyers had to quiz clients about their sex lives — and then duck! Some clients would become furious and blast their counsel for having the colossal nerve to ask such impudent questions. Fortunately, though, others came up with humorous remarks.

Kenneth C. Binks, Q.C., of Ottawa tells about a Toronto colleague who explained the foregoing to a woman who was suing for divorce.

"So you'll understand, Mrs. Jones, that I *have* to ask you this question," he said anxiously.

"Yes, I understand," she replied.

"Well, then, have you ever committed adultery yourself?"

"Do you mean with anyone other than your senior partner?" she inquired.

Let's pause here to get our signals straight.

"Hanky-panky," the subject of this learned essay, is a catchy little phrase that, alas, is often undervalued. When encountering this expression one always — and quite correctly — thinks of standard, garden-variety adultery. But the term "hanky-panky" has a much broader scope than that. It embraces all manner of extra-curricular amorous activities, conventional and otherwise. Yes, indeed, hanky-panky covers a multitude of sins.

Toronto lawyer Joel A. Kerbel reports:

"Some years ago I was retained in a divorce proceeding by a woman of few words from a rural community. She assured me that her husband was guilty of adultery — she had caught him in the act — and told him she would divorce him. She also assured me that he would admit the act in court.

"I took the usual particulars of the marriage, the present address of the parties (who lived on a farm), and the date of the adultery, which was allegedly committed in one of the farm's outbuildings.

"I then asked the name of the adultress.

"'Bessie,' said my client.

"'Last name?' I asked.

"'Don't have a last name,' was the reply.

"I continued making notes as to dates of birth, ages of the parties and their children, information about family assets, and near the end of the discussion I informed my client that it would be necessary to try to serve documents on the co-respondent. I said that to assist the sheriff in serving the papers it would be helpful to have any information we could get about the co-respondent's address, appearance or identity.

"'Oh, she lives on our farm,' my client said.

"'And you don't know her last name?' I asked.

"'Well, to tell you the truth,' she replied, 'we never give any of our cows last names.'"

Alexander S. Romanchuk, a lawyer in St. Albert, Alberta, reminisces about a memorable case:

"In the late 1960s, I acted for the plaintiff in a divorce case, a Ukrainian woman of very limited education. She and her husband, who was twenty years older than she, had a farm near a small town in northern Alberta.

"My client had a heavy, pronounced Ukrainian accent when she spoke English. During the pre-trial examination for discovery, I asked my opponent to please speak slowly and deliberately so that my client could understand her questions. The examination proceeded as follows:

Q. Now, ma'am, you had had supper and were washing the dishes.
A. Yeh.
Q. Where was your husband?
A. I saw him leave da house.
Q. Do you know where he went?
A. I don't know.
Q. What did he do then?
A. I went outside to look for him. It was dark.
Q. Did you find him?
A. Yeh.
Q. Where was he?
A. He was in da barn.
Q. What was he doing?

A. He was focking da cow.

"With that, my opponent jumped up in great astonishment and, in a quivering voice, pointed at me and said, digustedly, '*Mr. Romanchuk!*'

"I told her that it was not *me* 'focking da cow' and, with that, she packed her file, her briefcase, and her client and strode out of the examination room in quite a huff, leaving me, my client and the court reporter laughing hilariously.

"We had petitioned for divorce on the perfectly valid ground of bestiality, but when we saw it was such an embarrassment to counsel we switched to cruelty — using the same evidence, though — and got a decree of divorce on that ground."

Provincial Court Judge Pat Curran files this dispatch from Halifax:

"As you know, we have no caribou or elk in Nova Scotia. We do not, however, lack a rutting season.

"Sergeant John Smith [a cleverly-concocted alias] had been in the armed forces for twenty-five years. His duties had taken him all over the world. In the fall, he and his wife began to have marriage problems. In early November they decided to separate and Sergeant Smith moved out of the matrimonial home. Three days later he returned home, only to find his wife and another man 'embracing.' At least, that was how the Crown put it.

"When defense counsel rose, he said that the Crown had been too delicate, that it had told the truth, but not the whole truth. Mrs. Smith and friend were engaged in what you could say was a total embrace, while lying on the floor absolutely naked.

"When Sergeant Smith saw this, he became somewhat upset and thrashed both Mrs. Smith and friend. He was charged with assaulting the two of them. The original charge was assault causing bodily harm, but no harm was alleged and he was permitted to plead guilty to the offence of simple assault.

"Defense counsel recounted Sergeant Smith's many virtues, including his spotless record in the armed forces. In summing up and making a pitch for clemency, he said, 'Everything was going fine for my client until he got himself into a rut.'

"I could still hear antlers clashing on the mountainside when I finished sentencing him."

Victoria, British Columbia, lawyer J. Trevor Alexander has a story about a *real* Mr. Smith:

"Years ago, Hugh J. McGivern, Q.C., in a big heroin conspiracy trial in Vancouver, was cross-examining a Crown witness, Smith by name. Smith had RCMP authority to traffic in heroin and thereby gather evidence against the co-conspirators.

"He was warned that such activities could be physically ruinous but nonetheless remained totally unscathed. However, McGivern drew Smith's attention to an incident several years earlier when Smith had been shot by a jealous lover because of Smith's dalliance with that lover's lady friend.

"After showing that no harm had come to Smith during his drug-trafficking activities, McGivern turned to the jury and, with a shrug of his shoulders, exclaimed, 'Well, now, Mr. Smith, I suppose that the one lesson you've learned is that fucking is more dangerous than trafficking!'

"Everyone in the courtroom, including the judge and jury, collapsed in uncontrollable mirth."

David C. Day, Q.C., of St. John's, the bloke you met at the beginning of this chapter, has a couple more stories about the perils of hanky-panky.

"Not a few unmarried couples part company following a telephone call from the woman to the object of her affections, advising that she is experiencing unplanned, alarming physiological changes," Day writes. "In one such case, my client was, I concluded, a tout possessing remarkable sexual proclivities.

"The products of the woman's indiscriminate nocturnal activity were a pregnancy and considerable doubt about its author.

"She alleged paternity against a trolley-bus driver. He defended by leading evidence from six fellow trolley operators that she was carnally familiar with them all.

"Judge Charles L. Roberts invoked the 'possible fathers' provision of the *Children of Unmarried Parents Act* and declared *all seven* drivers liable to contribute to support of my client's offspring."

Toronto lawyer Garry K. Braund, Q.C., is an incurable ham — an allegation he'd readily admit.

Back in the 1960s, Garry represented a Niagara Falls couple who pleaded not guilty to charges of owning and operating a common bawdy house. The Crown Attorney presented a considerable amount of scientific evidence pertaining to traces of sperm found on bedsheets in the couple's home.

Cross-examining an "expert" witness on this subject, Braund asked: "Couldn't that just as easily be sperm from a dog as from humans?"

The witness said that was possible, but not likely.

For the next ten minutes, Braund peppered the witness with questions about dogs and the methods used to distinguish dog sperm from the sperm of humans — despite the fact that there was absolutely no evidence on the record that the accused owned a dog or had ever allowed one on the premises.

At one point Braund, amazed that he was getting so much mileage out of a mythical dog, brought the house down when he turned to his clients and rasped: "Woof! Woof!"

Until 1968, when divorce reform was unleashed across the land, adultery was virtually the only ground for divorce in Canada — except in Nova Scotia where, due to a pre-Confederation statute, cruelty was also recognized.

One day, in the early 1960s, the aforementioned Garry Braund acted for a Peterborough man who wanted to sue his wife for divorce. But first he had to "get the goods" on her — i.e., prove she'd committed adultery. The standard way of doing that in those days was to hire a private detective.

Barrister Braund brought in *two* private-eyes and told them to scoot up to Peterborough and lose no time in tracking down "the subject" — spy-talk for the party who's being tailed.

Being from Peterborough himself, and knowing the woman in question, Braund suggested that the dicks proceed directly to a certain downtown drinking establishment. "If you get talking to anyone, tell them you're in the insurance business," he said as they left his office.

The operatives had been in the pub only a few minutes when they spotted the subject and her boyfriend drinking at a nearby table. The couple saw the men looking their way and invited them to come over and join them. Such breaks do not usually occur so promptly in the snoop business.

After some preliminary chit-chat about insurance, the four of them had a jolly time until the lights started blinking and patrons were shown the door.

"Say, would you fellows like to join us for a nightcap at our apartment?" asked the subject.

"Sure," they responded, in unison. This was going to be a snap!

Following another hour of merriment, the visitors hit the road.

"We've had a great time," remarked one of them, "but it's well after two and we have a lot of insurance business to transact in the morning."

The men headed for the nearest phone and woke Garry Braund in Toronto.

"Is there a problem?" Braund asked one of the dicks, a colorful chap named Tom who called himself "The Bloodshot Eye That Never Sleeps."

"The problem is that this is getting embarrassing," Tom replied.

He told Braund about the fun time they'd had with the subject and her friend.

"We've gotten to know these people, Garry, and we really like them," Tom said. "It's going to be awfully tough to bust in on them now!"

"Duty calls, Tom," said Braund. "You've got to go through with it. That's what you're being paid for."

Braund said he'd call his client, the husband, who lived in Peterborough, and get him to join them at the scene of the crime.

About half an hour later the three men kicked in the apartment door and confronted the lovers, who were just finishing a nightcap of a different kind.

The aggrieved husband walked straight to the subject's side of the bed and inquired, "Cigarette, dear?"

Just shy of seventy, Douglas Hopkinson of Southampton, Ontario, calls himself "Canada's oldest practicing private investigator." Admiring friends and associates have another name for this relentless digger — "Dauntless Doug the Dick."

Off and on, but mostly on, Dauntless Doug has been involved in the national and international gumshoe trade since 1946. He once owned and operated the largest private investigation firm in Ontario, but he chucked it in 1972 because the strain of eighteen-hour workdays was making him jumpy and indecisive, and a bad health risk, to boot.

After a decade as an investigator with the Ontario Unemployment Insurance Commission, he retired again because of ill health. A few weeks later he had a stroke that took a couple of years or so to recuperate from and in 1986 he and his wife Flora moved to Southampton (population three thousand) on the shores of beautiful Lake Huron. Within a year he was back in business again, specializing in finding missing persons.

The heyday of the private-eye was the 1940s to the late 1960s, when "no-fault" divorce was ushered in, and if anyone can talk about those good-old-bad-old days it's Douglas Hopkinson, who's been involved in the investigation of over thirteen hundred cases of suspected hanky-panky. They produced more than a few laughs.

There was, for example, "The Great Medical Emergency Caper."

In 1969, Hopkinson was hired to get the dirt on a man who'd been carrying on an affair in a certain Toronto apartment. How to get into the apartment? That was the question.

Dress up — that was the answer.

Hopkinson had two law students working part-time for him, one of each sex, and he decided to manufacture a "medical emergency" that would get all three of them into the residence — the male student posing as a doctor, the woman student impersonating a nurse, and the boss passing himself off as an ambulance driver.

From a barber friend, Doug borrowed two barber's jackets — one for the "doctor" and the other for the "ambulance driver." He bought a cheap stethoscope from a medical supplies firm and told the "doctor" to make sure it dangled from one of the pockets of his nice white coat.

"I picked up a cheap black taxi driver's hat for myself at the Crippled Civilians outlet," Hopkinson recalls, "and for the 'nurse' I got a cheap hairdresser's smock from Kresge's, some cheap white shoes from Woolworth's, and a cheap badge, that looked like a nurse's pin, from a pawn shop. I then went to a nurses' supply store and got a pretty good price on a nurse's cap."

Decked out in their new duds, and carrying a stretcher, the trio made a bee-line for the apartment in question.

Hopkinson rapped hard and fast on the door.

"Who's there? What do you want?" came a male voice from the apartment.

"We're here from the hospital!" Hopkinson shouted, excitedly. "We're answering an emergency call!"

"Not here," replied the man inside. "There's no emergency here!"

"Oh, my God!" yelled Hopkinson. "They must have given us the wrong address! Somebody's waiting anxiously for us somewhere else — and we don't know where that is! This is a matter of life or death, sir! Please let us in so we can call the hospital and get the right address!"

A man with a towel wrapped around his waist opened the door — just as a nearly naked woman nipped into the bathroom and snapped the lock with all her might.

"Where's the phone? Where's the phone?" babbled Hopkinson as the emergency medical team ran into the apartment.

"It's in the bedroom," replied the man.

What a break! thought Hopkinson. We get to see the bedroom!

For evidentiary purposes, the intruders memorized almost everything they saw in the boudoir — the disheveled bed, the liquor bottles, the undies strewn here and there, the jar of petroleum jelly on the floor beside the bed.

The "doctor" faked a call to the hospital and got "the right number."

"Sorry to bother you, sir," he said as he and his helpers left the apartment.

"That's all right," the man replied. "Good luck with your patient!"

Another time, Doug Hopkinson was hired by the wife of a Toronto lawyer who was gliding around with a ballet dancer. He knew this lawyer, who'd used his services in cases of his own.

It was an easy investigation. Hopkinson followed the couple to a motel and saw them register and go to their room. From his vantage point he could see everything that happened through the drapes, at least while the lights were on. When the lights went out he followed standard private-eye procedure — he waited several hours, knocked on the door, gave the man his card, then left and reported to his client.

"He's at it again," the lawyer's wife told Hopkinson six months later. She'd reconciled with her husband after the earlier episode.

When Dauntless Doug heard this news, it was coming up for the supper hour. He wanted to make sure that Loverboy remained in the office long enough for him to get down there and follow him when he left. So he called the lawyer and, in a fake Italian accent, he said he was anxious to see him and retain his services in an upcoming divorce case.

"I'm on my way now," said the bogus Italian. Then, realizing that that wouldn't necessarily keep the lawyer there, he added a few words that probably would: "I only have three thousand dollars on me, but I can get more for you later."

The lawyer stayed in his office until seven-thirty and Hopkinson tailed him from the moment he left.

History repeated itself. The subject picked up the same ballerina and took her to the same motel, where they got the same room as before. And at 4:00 A.M. Hopkinson knocked on the door and gave the subject his card. "I'm getting sick of seeing you!" the man remarked.

The private-eye reported back to his client, who, once again, reconciled with her husband.

A few weeks later, the lawyer's wife retained Hopkinson for a third time. She said she's been tipped off that the next night her husband would be rooming with the dancer at the Chateau Laurier Hotel in Ottawa. In a flash, Hopkinson was off for the nation's capital.

He was there when the lovebirds arrived and, hiding behind a potted palm, he overheard them being assigned to room 721.

As soon as they'd disappeared, Hopkinson asked the desk clerk if he could please have room 723.

"It's my favorite room," he said. "It holds a lot of wonderful memories for me."

His wish granted, the operative set up shop in room 723. He removed the wall-plate from a socket and inserted a miniature microphone connected to a tape recorder with earphones. When that didn't give the greatest reception he employed his emergency equipment — an electronic stethoscope embedded in the hole at the top of the suction-cup of a toilet plunger — and he was able to hear every amorous word that was being whispered on the other side of the wall.

At 5:00 A.M., Hopkinson knocked on the door.

"Good morning, sir," he said to the subject, for the third time. "Here's my card. I suggest you get yourself a good lawyer. You're going to need one."

"I have only two words for you," replied the subject. "Fuck off!"

This time, the wife proceeded with the case. She had three times as much evidence as she needed.

Back in 1969, Doug Hopkinson was retained by the wife of a corporate executive who was cheating on her night after night in his girlfriend's apartment atop a fifteen-storey building.

"I love a challenge," Doug says, "but this was ridiculous. There was no vantage point anywhere in the vicinity. Short of my being *in* the apartment, the only way I could get any evidence would be if someone held me by my ankles from the roof and I was lucky enough to get a photograph through the window.

"I phoned a fellow private-eye in Hamilton," Hopkinson says. "He was a massive man, a former steelworker who was six foot six and weighed 350 pounds. He was as strong as an ox and he had these enormous paws."

The next night, the two men went out on the roof of the building. Clasping his flash-camera, Hopkinson lay partially over the edge of the roof, sixteen storeys above the ground, and the giant seized him by the ankles with his vise-like hands and then dangled his 200-pound body in front of the penthouse window.

As luck would have it, the lovers were in. Not only that, but they were buck naked and doing rather licentious things to each other — right in front of the window.

"I got a great shot that we used later in court," Hopkinson relates. "It clinched the case!"

"You must have been terrified," I said.

"I was," said Dauntless Doug, "especially right after I took the photograph."

"What happened then?" I asked.

"When my friend was yanking me up, I felt his thumb slip over the stocking on my right ankle!"

Thomas A. Newman, Q.C., of Pickering, Ontario, writes:

"Many years ago, I attended at the sittings in Whitby on what seemed to be a routine divorce application.

"During the actual trial, it had become obvious that all three parties to the divorce action were from Newfoundland and that all the matters of consequence had taken place in Newfoundland.

"After the decree *nisi* was granted, I made application on behalf of the respondent to have the decree made absolute at trial upon what seemed to be very reasonable grounds. The respondent was pregnant and she and the co-respondent wished to be married before the child was born.

"The judge proceeded to question the respondent and the co-respondent as to what led up to the respondent's condition. During this examination, it became apparent, as I already knew, that the respondent had slept with the co-respondent on only one occasion, at the respondent's parents' cottage.

"The judge then asked the respondent the fatal question — where in Newfoundland was she from?

"'Conception Bay,' she answered.

"With a somewhat whimsical smile on his face, His Lordship then asked the respondent where the co-respondent was from.

"'Come-by-Chance', she said."

13

MISCELLANEOUS MERRIMENT

LAUGHTER IS THE CLOSEST THING TO THE GRACE OF GOD.

Karl Barth

You never know who you'll run into in a courthouse. Just ask the Honorable Noel H. Goodridge, Chief Justice of Newfoundland. He has a reminiscence that's positively divine:

"As a lawyer I represented in court a young boy who was injured in an automobile accident. He was accompanied at the trial by his father. They were late in arriving at court after the lunch recess.

"While I was trying to appease the presiding judge over the delay, the two appeared. The father came into court first, followed by his son and, moments later, another man, apparently a grandfather of the injured boy, who was old, gaunt, cadaverous, and pale.

"On the appearance of the first two in court, I said, somewhat relieved, to the judge, 'Here come the father and the son.' When the other man came into court behind them, the court clerk muttered, 'And here comes the Holy Ghost.'"

Toronto lawyer Paul Calarco files this report:

"Recently I was engaged in prosecuting drug offenses in the District Court in Toronto. I was, of course, fully gowned and, as is my habit, was wearing black pants with the gown. I am six foot one, weigh two hundred pounds, and have dark curly hair and a Fu Manchu mustache.

"I must have been looking particularly sinister that day since, as I passed a toddler, perhaps three years old, the child looked at me and ran over to his mother. He pointed at me and asked his mom, 'Is that the Devil?'"

Mr. Justice Melvin E. Shannon of the Court of Queen's Bench of Alberta advises that on October 20, 1989, he was "required to sit in judgment in a contest between God and the Devil."

James Jutzi pleaded not guilty to a charge of breaking into the apartment of Bryant Sallenbach and assaulting him.

Sallenbach testified that he was watching TV in his apartment when the accused, "a madman," knocked down his front door, "broke it right off its hinges," and "started hitting me on the head." He said he sustained a black eye and a cut that required several stitches.

When Crown Counsel asked him, "How long have you known this man?" Sallenbach replied, "I've known him as he looks, someone that looks like him, for a couple of years."

We turn now to the court-certified transcript of the trial to see how the complainant fared when he was cross-examined by defense counsel Barbara D. Janusz:

Q. Mr. Sallenbach, what did you mean that you have known him for a couple of years as he looks? You stated in examination-in-chief that you have known him as he looks for a couple of years. What did you mean by that?

A. Well, being the God of eternal truth, I have in the past few years done some powerful things, and I have trapped the Evil One who has lived in the year 1980 — the Evil One, the Devil, Satan, Lucifer. And he has, in invisible ways and physical ways, been quite a nuisance in my life. I am the only one who could do that, with the invisibleness of my powers of death and the force that is invisible in the Almighty, in the nimbus that protects me, in the invisibleness of my being. And I have noticed changes throughout my life historically about people who did not have the wisdom to fear me and my invisible powers of death and eternal damnation — things like that. And it's been inconvenient sometimes, but it's about dealing with that stuff being me.

Q. Are you suggesting that this evil nuisance is what caused this to happen on March the eighteenth, 1989?

A. It's bound to be a part of that, you know, related in some way.

Q. So, you're suggesting, sir, that it was some evil force that knocked the door down in your own apartment?

A. Using him as the instrument, yes, absolutely, unmistakably, no doubt, undeniably true.

Sallenbach said that "he" had also broken down his door the year before.

Q. And when you are saying "he," you are saying this evil force again?

A. Yes, this —

Q. This evil force.

A. — evil man, yes. A disciple of the Devil, to be sure, card-carrying, to be sure, guaranteed. This is the word from the God of eternal truth, speaking the fullness of truth now.

THE ACCUSED: Excuse me.

Q. So you are saying that the Devil did this on a previous occasion and on March the eighteenth, 1989?

A. Yes, through him, umm-hmm.

A Calgary police officer testified that when he went to the apartment about 8:00 A.M. the next day, Sallenbach had a black eye but his glasses were in good condition.

"When I entered the apartment," he said, "the apartment door itself was leaning against a wall just inside the apartment. It had been knocked or taken right off the hinges." He said the door was made of solid wood and weighed about sixty pounds. He also stated: "I was satisfied that what he told me that morning had indeed happened."

Q. Did you make inquiries of the tenants in the building as to whether they heard anything the night before?

A. Yes, I did. The tenant who would be to the left of Mr. Sallenbach's apartment, I had spoken to him briefly, and he said he did hear a commotion coming from Mr. Sallenbach's apartment, two men yelling and screaming.

Q. But he didn't tell you that he came out and took a look at who was —

A. Not that I can recall, no. He just heard a commotion.

The accused testified that he'd had religious arguments with Sallenbach in the past ("This man is trying to tell me he's God?") and he stated emphatically that he'd never been at his place nor caused him any kind of harm.

On cross-examination, the accused admitted that a year or so before he'd been confined in a mental hospital, but he said that was due to a misunderstanding. "I didn't consider myself God at any time," he said. "A lady misunderstood me when I said I believed that I am a son of the living God, a Christian, a son of the living God."

In argument, defense counsel Barbara Janusz stated: "My Lord, I would submit that the Crown has failed to prove beyond a reasonable doubt that Mr. Jutzi attended on March the eighteenth at the residence of Bryant Sallenbach and committed an assault. Mr. Sallenbach believes that he is God and that my client is the Devil. . . . Mr. Sallenbach recalls an incident, but he seems to be rather confused and believes that it was an evil force that came in the door and states that it was in the form of this man."

Crown Counsel Elizabeth A. Miller agreed that "it's a matter of one person's word against another," but she said that the complainant, though "suffering from some delusions," was "quite articulate" about what had happened.

In giving judgment, Mr. Justice Shannon stated:

"The Crown presents one witness only to establish the guilt of the accused, and that is the complainant. There is no confirming or corroborating evidence. . . .

"The victim says that he is the God of eternal truth, and this court has no way of knowing whether that is true or not, but in the view of this court he does suffer from some kind of delusions; and this court does not have sufficient confidence in his testimony to enable it to convict the accused. Consequently, it must give the benefit of the doubt to the accused.

"Stand up, Mr. Jutzi. I find you not guilty."

In a letter to me, His Lordship added this tongue-in-cheek postscript to the proceedings: "My wife tells me that she was not surprised that I acquitted 'the Devil.'"

We move now to another eerie subject — voices from beyond.

Vancouver lawyer Terence La Liberté sent me a dandy transcript from the Bella Bella — Bella Coola Court circuit in the hinterlands of northern British Columbia. Before we take a squint at it, though, let's get some background from Terry:

"The court team travels into the Indian village of Bella Bella and the small community of Bella Coola every couple of months. In Bella Bella, the court is held on the Indian reserve, in the United Church. Our court clerks use a Uher tape recorder that, once plugged into the Bella Bella power supply, tends to pick up interference from the Canadian Broadcasting Company.

"On the date in question, CBC Radio broadcast a talk-show on the subject of 'Cold Turkey Day' and the callers were apparently discussing their problems with smoking. The court reporter can usually hear these interceptions through the head sets, and in the past we've had to utilize other power sources. However, when the reporter returned to Vancouver the excerpt enclosed was 'captured' on her tape.

"The presiding judge was C. C. Barnett of Williams Lake, B.C. Anthony J. Rowley, from Sechelt, B.C., was provincial Crown Counsel and Lisa Dewar, from Mission, B.C., was the defense lawyer. I appear on the circuit representing the federal Crown."

According to the transcript, here's what was said at the opening of court in Bella Bella, B.C., on January 23, 1987:

MR. ROWLEY: Calling number one, Richard Taylor.
CBC RADIO: . . . finally, ten years later, I quit smoking.
MS. DEWAR: Appearing as agent for Mr. Taylor.
CBC RADIO: . . . the only time I really want one is after good sex.
THE COURT: There'll be a warrant.

Terry La Liberté has another classic story from the circuit:

"It isn't always counsel who are green, and it isn't only Rodney Dangerfield who 'don't get no respect.'

"On a few of our court trips to northern B.C., several years ago, our regular judge was replaced by different judges from around the province. On one such occasion, a relatively new appointment decided he would wear his equally new judicial robe to show the appropriate respect for our surroundings in the United Church, where we hold court in Bella Bella.

"We had placed the judge's bench on the raised platform that serves as an altar in the center of the room, and the spectators were seated all around him. His Honor was indeed splendid as he dispensed justice to the multitudes.

"A young native boy of about four or five years of age was seated 'at the right hand of the father' [the judge, that is] and he looked up in awe as His Honor pronounced a judgment.

"Court clerk Molly Carroll and I caught each other's eyes as the tyke reached over, very unconsciously, and wiped his nose with the hem of the judge's robe. I thought Molly was going to hemorrhage, she was laughing so hard."

La Liberté chuckles when he recalls an impaired-driving case in Bella Coola:

"In May of 1979 we were trying to get the new Legal Aid duty counsel in Bella Bella a little credibility with the locals, who are often wary of a new face in town. His case was uphill, to say the least, but he took up the challenge splendidly.

"If convicted, his man was going to go to jail for a while, so the lawyer argued with great vigor. He kept the entire gallery spellbound at his rhetoric and his zeal.

"About three-quarters of the way through his address, a young woman very quietly and meekly came forward and placed a suitcase next to the accused. Counsel looked down and, without skipping a beat, said, 'Somehow, I don't think they have much confidence in my argument.'

"Court had to stand down for a few minutes because Judge Cunliffe Barnett was laughing so hard."

Seven months later, the same fellow had another trial before Judge Cunliffe Barnett. This time he was charged with attempting to break into the Bella Coola liquor store, located just a bottle's throw from the local detachment of the RCMP

"In those days," says Judge Barnett, "a junior member of the detachment had quarters in the detachment building. About 3:00 A.M., he was wakened by loud noises coming from the vicinity of the liquor store. He dressed and went there.

"He found the accused, well known to him, at the rear of the store, bashing away at the barred window with a wrecking bar.

"'What are you doing, Craig?' the officer inquired.

"'What do you *think* I'm doing?' the man replied. 'I'm trying to get booze. Geez, I should've brought dynamite — this place is built like a fuckin' fortress!'

"This statement was admitted into evidence and, once again, Craig enjoyed the pleasure of Her Majesty's hospitality."

Jil McIntosh of Oshawa, Ontario, has a story about some other folks who talked themselves into trouble:

"One day in 1977, I accompanied a friend who was summoned to appear in court in Burlington on a charge of careless driving. While we were waiting, two men were called up who'd been stopped by local police for picking up a rabbit they'd run over. It was illegal to pick up any kind of 'road kill.'

"The men had explained to the officer that they were hunters, and they said they'd picked up the dead rabbit in order to bait their traps with it. Picking up the rabbit was punishable by a fine of only fifteen dollars or so, but they said they were innocent trappers and to prove it they took the policeman to the back of their van to show him that what they were *really* out for was wild game.

"They opened the van and proudly showed him that day's catch — three Canada geese, which are, of course, protected by law. That earned them a hefty fine *and* a jail term."

That reminds me of a heart-tugging story sent to me recently by noted Regina lawyer — and fellow author — Morris C. Shumiatcher, Q.C. Here it is, just as he wrote it:

"A sad-eyed gentleman appeared before a judge in an undisclosed jurisdiction, charged with destroying a protected bird. A condor.

"Contrite and humble, the accused advised the court that it was true, that he had, in fact, shot and killed a condor, and that, indeed, it was a protected bird.

"'However,' he said, 'there are extenuating circumstances. My wife and I and our three small children spent all winter in a cabin, high in the mountains. Our food ran out; we could not leave. We faced starvation.

"'Providence brought sudden succor. A huge bird — a condor — appeared on the rooftop of our hut. It was a sign from heaven. It meant life for us. I took my gun and I shot the bird. We prepared it, cooked it and ate it and, indeed, it saved the lives of all five of us. If it were not for that bird, which gave life to us, I would not be here today. Nor would my family be alive!'

"The judge was duly impressed. He pondered the facts and he held that the conservation laws had, indeed, been breached. But only out of necessity. This was a full and complete defense. The accused was discharged.

"The grateful man thanked the judge profusely. He bowed and was about to leave the courtroom when the judge called to him and said, 'By the way, sir, I am curious, tell me — what does condor really taste like?'

"The accused hesitated. 'Well,' he replied, 'it tastes pretty much like a cross between a bald eagle and a whooping crane.'"

David G. Lawrence, a Toronto lawyer who has a keen interest in military law, files this report from the front:

"A young officer attending a court-martial during World War I was asked by the presiding Judge Advocate General what he thought the sentence should be for a soldier who had just been found guilty of cowardice in the face of the enemy.

"'I suggest that he be confined to barracks for fourteen days,' the officer replied.

"The Judge Advocate General exploded: 'Fourteen days C.B.? Fourteen days C.B.? Good Lord, man, the maximum sentence for this offense is *death*!'

"'I'm sorry, sir,' the young man said, 'I hadn't realized that. Then I suggest death.'"

Ronald R. Jeffels of Richmond, British Columbia, sure has a way with words:

"In a previous incarnation I was an officer in Double-Yew Double-Yew Two. I used to muck about with courts-martial and I got to know the *Manual of Military Law* better than most men know the lobes of their wives' ears. After all, if you're a criminal by training and predilection, you have to take measures to protect yourself.

"In Britain I once defended a trooper — a real knuckles-in-the-dust type — on a double paternity charge. And that's not all. The objects of his search for immortality through seminal propagation were mother and daughter.

"Mum worked the day shift in the munitions plant; daughter toiled by night in the same locale. My trooper worked every shift: he was in and out of the bed like a fiddler's elbow. And what follows is true (I swear by gods foreign and domestic!) — both women produced their offspring on the same day in the same hospital.

"I'm not going to boggle your mind by tracing the consanguinity involved in the relationship and, more particularly, the relationship of daughter's baby to mother's baby to mother's husband, who was trying to help Montgomery defeat Rommel in the desert.

"The presiding Judge Advocate General was wise and charitable. He posted my trooper back to Canada as an instructor in small arms at Petawawa. He told *me* to get lost."

An Alberta judge, who shall remain nameless because his wife thinks he doesn't know any naughty words, told me a wonderful military/legal yarn from Double-Yew Double-Yew Two. His Lordship heard the story in the late 1940s, when, as an articled law student, he worked for a lawyer who'd done legal work on the case in question. Here's the tale he was told by his boss just two or three years after the latter had returned from the wars:

In Britain, near the end of hostilities, two Canadian soldiers pleaded not guilty to a charge of rape. One of them testified that they met a prostitute "in a fuckin' bar" and bought her "a fuckin' drink."

"What happened then?" asked their lawyer.

"We asked her what her fuckin' price was," the soldier replied, "and then we bought her a couple more fuckin' drinks and then we left the fuckin' pub and walked down the fuckin' street with her."

"Yes, then what?"

"We crossed the fuckin' street, climbed over a fuckin' fence, and went into a fuckin' field."

"What happened then?"

"An act of intercourse took place."

There's nothing inherently funny about drinking and driving, what with all the injuries, deaths, and destruction that can flow therefrom. But laughter lurks everywhere, even in that sad sphere of human transgression, and every now and then something humorous is said in the course of a drinking-driving investigation.

Judge Harold Gyles of the Provincial Court of Manitoba has a slew of stories about the "bad old days," before breathalyzer tests were made mandatory in cases of suspected impaired driving.

"Back then," he says, "the suspect practically had to be holding onto the grass so he wouldn't roll off the world before an accused could be convicted of driving while impaired."

Judge Gyles recalls a case in which an RCMP officer testified that he stopped a motorist after seeing his car weaving over the center-line of the highway.

The accused lowered his window and the officer said, "Let me see your driver's licence."

The man dropped his wallet on the floor of the car, fumbled for it, found it after a great deal of groping, and then extracted a card for the policeman.

"Why, when I asked you for your driver's licence, did you give me your Manitoba Medical card?" the officer inquired.

"Because," said the fast-thinking suspect, "I thought I'd give you something to read while I looked for my driver's licence."

In another drinking-driving case in the pre-breathalyzer era, Judge Gyles says that a Brandon man was, in effect, rewarded for his sense of humor.

"A policeman saw this fellow lose control of his car, drive over the median and then, amazingly, steer a slalom course through a grove of trees," His Honor reports.

"Have you been drinking?" the policeman asked when he caught up with the motorist.

"Of course I've been drinking!" the man replied. "What the fuck do you think I am, a stunt driver?"

The cop laughed so hard he didn't lay a charge.

Sharon Gately, a court reporter in Whitehorse, reports that in a recent impaired driving case in that Yukon city it was disclosed that when the accused went to the breathalyzer machine he took the mouthpiece and started talking into it.

"Hello, hello," he said, "this is Mr. Smith. Is anybody there?"

Not long ago, a Montreal businessman, after having a few snorts with some friends, decided to call it a day and drive home. Along the way, he was stopped for a spot-check by police. The constable who detained him detected the smell of alcohol and so he asked him to step out of his vehicle.

During the investigation, the officer's attention was diverted to another matter. A few moments later, the detainee decided he wasn't going to wait around any longer — so he got behind the wheel and drove off.

When he arrived home he instructed his wife that if the police should come to the door she was to say he was asleep in bed.

Shortly thereafter, a policeman knocked at the door and asked to see the man of the house. When he was told he was asleep, the officer insisted he was to be wakened.

The man shuffled to the front door and the officer asked him where he'd been that evening. He said he'd been home all night, asleep in bed.

"Where's your car?" the policeman asked.

"In the garage."

"Will you please let me have a look at it?"

"Certainly. Follow me."

The man opened his garage door and there it was — a police cruiser, complete with siren and flashing lights.

Ever wonder where criminal lawyers get some of their dingbat clients? Read on.

District Court Judge Spyros D. Loukidelis of Sudbury has a story about a couple of stick-up "artists" who were prosecuted by a friend of his in British Columbia.

"Two robbers drove into a small shopping plaza. They got out of their car and crouched down behind it to put on stocking-masks. When they stood up they realized that they had their masks on backwards.

"They eventually solved that problem and went into a Singer Sewing Center and announced that this was a bank robbery. The lady told them that the bank was two doors down. They thanked her and went into the bank.

"One of them stood guard and his partner explained to a young teller that this was a robbery and they wanted money. She fearfully complied. He then looked around and said to the teller that the bag to carry the loot in had been left in the car and would she please lend them a bag. She complied.

"The two rushed out of the bank and the alarm was rung by the staff. The man who'd gotten the money had to return as he'd left the car keys on the counter. He then rushed out to join his companion just as the police arrived. There was a shoot-out and one of the two was wounded before they surrendered."

Listen up, landlubbers, Mr. Justice Seamus B. O'Regan of the Supreme Court of Newfoundland has a nautical yarn for you:

"A well-known town drunk appeared in Provincial Court in St. John's on a charge of being drunk in public.

"Two rookie police officers testified that they had arrested the accused while he was staggering east on Water Street.

"The defendant took the stand and stated that he was not drunk on the night in question and, contrary to what the police officers said, he was walking west on Water Street when he was arrested.

"On cross-examination, the defendant, who made every attempt to be cooperative with the court, stated that he *could* have been walking east on Water Street. He went on to state that he was walking east for a while, then west, then east, then west, then east, then west, but he was quite sure that when he was arrested he was walking west on Water Street.

"Enjoying the game, the Provincial Court judge asked the defendant for a further explanation of the evidence relating to east and west.

"At this stage, one of the court officials, who was a seasoned police veteran putting in his time before retirement, was heard to mutter in a voice loud enough for all to hear: 'Last night was very windy. I'm sure he was tacking.'"

Mr. Justice O'Regan also tells about a case he prosecuted in his lawyering days:

"A few years ago, a woman in Newfoundland was charged with the murder of her husband. The incident occurred in a small village consisting of approximately twenty families.

"The woman had shot her husband in his bed and claimed the defense of accident. Immediately after the shooting, she had run to one of her neighbors seeking assistance. The room was quickly filled with all of the people in the community, and it was obvious that the victim was dying.

"Describing the scene, one of the witnesses said that he heard the wife muttering outside the bedroom door:

"'What's I gonna do? What's I gonna do? What's I gonna do?'

"Continuing his evidence, the witness said that he heard the dying husband respond.

"Strictly speaking, that is hearsay and therefore inadmissible in evidence — unless the judge is satisfied, after hearing all the facts surrounding the event, that the words were spoken by the victim when he was dying and *knew* that he was dying.

"In the absence of the jury, the judge conducted a 'trial within a trial' on that vital issue and, in the end, he was satisfied that the man's utterance was a 'dying declaration' and so could properly be introduced in evidence.

"The jury was now permitted to hear what the dying man said in response to his wife's mutterings, which was:

"'What's *youse* gonna do? What's *I*'se a gonna do!'"

The Honorable Allan McEachern, Chief Justice of British Columbia, relates a revealing story from a civil court:

"Mr. Justice William Esson heard a personal injury claim with a jury. The plaintiff's complaint was an allegedly severe low back injury, which made it necessary always to sit on a special cushion with his back properly supported by an attachment to this cushion.

"Counsel for the plaintiff made a great fuss, both while the plaintiff was in the courtroom and in the witness box, about the plaintiff's dependence upon the cushion.

"The jury returned an unusually generous damage award, having apparently been satisfied that the plaintiff indeed had a serious back problem.

"Guess what the clerk found abandoned in the courtroom at the end of the trial. That's right — the indispensible cushion."

Donald M. Cooper, Q.C., of Yellowknife, Northwest Territories, recalls the time that a judge's wife, while her husband was in court, was invited into the mess of a Ministry of Transport base in Resolute Bay:

"As was the custom of all who entered that hallowed place, she was invited to kiss the 'Golden Ushuk,' a foot-long projection that resembled a night-stick. This she did happily.

"A few moments later, her husband entered the mess and was advised as to what had taken place. Red-faced, he explained to his wife that an ushuk was, in fact, a walrus's penis.

"Within easy earshot of those assembled, she was heard to remark, 'Lucky lady walrus!'"

Mr. Justice Patrick Galligan of the Supreme Court of Ontario reports that in a case he was involved in recently "one of the lawyers said that part of the style of cause [the name of the case] made him think 'wistfully' of times gone by."

In condensed form, the case answered to the name of *Hillis and Wroblewski versus Rapid Erection Scaffolds Ltd.*

Case names often reflect the subject matter of the case. For example, an Ontario annulment case based on non-consummation of the marriage was called *Doolittle verus Doolittle*. An Ontario divorce case, based on the adultery of one of the parties, was recorded in the law books as *Love versus Love and Dove*. Another Ontario case, having to do with wife-swapping, was known as *Goodfriend versus Goodfriend*.

A hotly contested Alberta case, where the court had to wrestle with the division of assets on the breakup of a marriage, was called *Hassell versus Hassell*. And a similar case in British Columbia is shown in court records as *Haaf versus Haaf*. In the realm of criminal law, a Vancouver case in which a prostitute told an undercover cop, "I give one terrific blow-job," can be found in volume 36 of the third series of Canadian Criminal Cases. It's called *The Queen versus Head.*

There's an ancient principle of law that reads, "*De minimis non curat lex*," which in English means, "The law does not concern itself with trifles."

Provincial Court Judge James D. Greco of Sault Ste. Marie, Ontario, recently heard a case in which a fisherman was charged with stealing three minnows from a fellow angler. His Honor dismissed the charge, stating for the record: "*De* minnows *non curat lex.*"

In another case that came before Judge Greco, a man was charged with the theft of two drill-bits. The accused requested an adjournment so he could secure the assistance of an interpreter.

"I'm going to adjourn this two-bit case until Friday," said Judge Greco, "so the accused can get an interpreter."

Guelph, Ontario, lawyer Joseph J. Berry well recalls one of his first appearances in court. When he was an articled law student in Ottawa, his boss sent him to Magistrate's Court to cop a quick plea for a client on a rather minor charge.

"Your Worship," said the greenhorn, "my instructions are to plead the accused guilty and ask for a fine."

"You better wait till they read the charge," advised Magistrate Glen Strike. "It might be murder."

Harry W. How, who retired recently as Chief Judge of the Provincial Court of Nova Scotia, tells about a Cape Breton woman who was charged with refusing to take a breathalyzer test:

"The nub of the defense was that the accused was not physically able to blow hard enough to take the test. The defense lawyer elicited from the police witness that the required breath sample was the equivalent of blowing up a balloon.

"Counsel produced a balloon and asked his client to inflate it. Sure enough, she couldn't. On cross-examination, she was asked to try it again and, to the consternation of her lawyer, she found the breath to inflate it fully. She was convicted.

"After court, the lawyer told the judge, 'I thought we had a great defense, but my client blew it!'"

On a bitterly cold winter's day in northern British Columbia, an RCMP constable on patrol came across a motorcyclist stalled by the roadside who was swathed in protective clothing and helmet.

"What's the matter?" the constable asked.

"Carburetor's frozen."

"Just piss on it. That'll thaw it out."

"I can't."

"Okay, I will."

The constable whipped out his instrument and peed all over the carburetor. The bike started and the rider drove off.

A few days later, the detachment office received a note of thanks from the father of the motor-bike rider. It began:

"On behalf of my daughter who recently was stranded . . ."

14

AND NOW A FEW WORDS FROM THE ACCUSED

LET HIM NOW SPEAK, OR ELSE HEREAFTER

FOR EVER HOLD HIS PEACE.

Book of Common Prayer

Facing the music is no frolic. Far from it.

"The criminal court is the most sorrowful place on earth," wrote British magistrate J. A. R. Cairns, back in the 1930s.

His Worship certainly knew whereof he spoke. His classic book on this grim subject, *The Loom of the Law*, contains these three powerful — and basically, still accurate — paragraphs:

"This, then, is the loom of the law, and its threads are human souls. Into the texture of its weavings are woven threads of many colours, white and gold, black and crimson and grey. It is a fabric of joy and sorrow, of laughter and tears, and across it breaks at times the sunshine of children's faces and sometimes the shadows of women's broken hearts.

"The loom has been built piece by piece throughout long generations. It is a vast complex machine of infinite parts, and it bears the impress of manifold limitations. It is called upon to do dreadful things. In the sorting of its threads it probes into the deepest depths of the human soul. It dissects the emotions, it lays bare the human heart and cuts it bit by bit. It weaves the thread of love and hate, of lust and greet, and its beams are often stained with the crimson of human blood.

"The loom kills men, and it breaks the hearts of women and makes orphans of unborn children. Every living soul is within the reach of its machinery, and you and I may be of its weaving tomorrow. Men are struck dumb with dismay, and women blind with grief. As we watch it day by day the problems of life grow into a vast, blinding, bewildering perplexity. Who knows his destiny? A frailty, a hidden vice, a secret sin, the weakness of a moment: 'Then comes the mist of the blinding rain/And life is never the same again.'"

Wow!

Enough of this stark reality! Let's have a look at the other side of the coin.

I present herewith a motley crew of accused persons who, wittingly or unwittingly, brought the blessed balm of laughter to the courtroom. Here, and in the hereafter, they should get time off for good behaviour.

Ottawa lawyer Kenneth C. Binks, Q.C., recalls a repeater who was about to be sentenced in the nation's capital.

"I should send you to the penitentiary," Judge Joachim Sauvé told the man in the dock, "but I'm going to send you to reformatory again.

"I see by your record that I sentenced you to penitentiary before. I did that for a purpose, you know — so that you could learn a trade. Why didn't you practice the trade they taught you?"

"Your Honor," the man replied, "did you ever try to get a job making licence plates?"

Willie Johnson was another fellow who'd been in and out of court a lot. One day, a few years ago, Willie was arraigned in a Texas courtroom on a felony charge.

The court clerk intoned: "The State of Texas versus Willie Johnson!" And before he could read further, the accused convulsed everyone within earshot by bellowing: "Lawd Gawd! What a majority!"

David Brisbin, an RCMP officer in Emerson, Manitoba, remembers a case in which a man who'd just pleaded guilty to a charge was asked by the judge, "What do you think I should do with you?"

"I don't know," said the culprit, "that's what they pay *you* for!"

"How do you plead to the charge?" the judge asked another old hand. "Are you guilty or not guilty?"

"How should I know?" asked the accused. "I haven't heard the evidence yet."

In another courtroom, the clerk read out a charge and asked the accused, "How do you plead to this charge, guilty or not guilty?"

The man didn't answer, so the judge barked, "How do you plead?"

"On bended knee, Your Honor," came the reply.

Claresholm, Alberta, lawyer Donald J. Welbourn files this report on a local prisoner at the bar:

"The well-dressed businessman was obviously ill at ease in the dock.

"The court clerk read out the formal charge of communicating for sexual purposes and then asked for a plea. The accused looked even more uncomfortable now, and he hesitated.

"'Come, come,' urged the judge, 'we must have your plea.'

"'My plea,' said the man, 'is that my wife doesn't find out about this.'"

Don Welbourn also has another story from his neck of the woods:

"The judge was being urged to grant an unconditional discharge to the clean-cut young first offender who'd just been convicted of robbing a convenience store.

"After hearing defense counsel extol his client's previously fine character, his evident remorsefulness, and the absence of violence during the commission of the offense, His Honor then asked the accused if he had anything to say before being sentenced.

"'Sure,' came the reply, 'those dumb cops never would've caught me if I hadn't tripped in the dark and lost my knife.'

"Needless to say, the discharge was denied."

Bert Lerch, of Neustadt, Ontario, reminisced with me recently about a man who'd been known to autograph checks that turned out to be null and void. One day, in the early 1950s, he was haled into court in Guelph for allowing two more negotiable instruments to bounce around the local landscape.

The accused pleaded guilty and the magistrate imposed a fine of fifty dollars on each charge, to be paid then and there, with the option of a month's stay in the county jail.

"Your Honor," said the condemned man, "I haven't got the cash, but I can give you a check."

Carl Morgan, editor of the Windsor (Ontario) *Star*, wrote to me concerning one of the first cases he covered as a cub reporter, in Trenton, Ontario, circa 1951.

"The accused was a notorious local fish poacher, a man who had been poaching in the Trent Canal waterways for years and almost always eluded the wardens," Carl reports. "That is the way he made his living, and he usually only took a nominal amount of fish at any one time.

"The problem was that he was growing deaf with age and had to take someone with him who could hear the approach of the wardens. This time he'd gone on his own and they'd sneaked up on him and bagged him and his catch."

The fellow pleaded guilty and the magistrate imposed a pretty stiff sentence for those days: "One hundred dollars or twenty days."

"I don't want to go to jail, but I don't have enough money to pay," said the accused.

"How much time do you need?" asked the magistrate.

"Well, Your Worship, that depends," the man replied. "If the whitefish are runnin' real good, I can pay it off by Friday."

Chief Judge Hazen Strange of the Provincial Court of New Brunswick told me a gripping tale when I was in his fair province in 1989. It concerns a teenaged motorist who was charged with squealing his tires — said dastardly offense having been committed on the night of the annual high-school formal dance.

The case was heard in a tiny New Brunswick town.

When all the sordid details of the case had been presented in evidence, the lad threw himself on the mercy of the court, proclaiming with great passion:

"I probably did squeal my tires, Your Honor, but I didn't do it on purpose. I'd just pulled up to the gym when I looked down and noticed that I had my old sneakers on — and the prom had already started.

"You see, Your Honor, this was a very formal dance. I had to get home as soon as possible to put on my *new* sneakers."

Also in 1989, Provincial Court Judge Pat Curran filed this lunar dispatch from Halifax:

"Recently, a man pleaded guilty before me to a charge of indecent exposure. According to the Crown, the defendant had been the passenger in a car that came up beside another car on a four-lane highway. The occupants of the second vehicle were a husband and wife and their young son.

"The Crown said that, after attracting the attention of his victims in the other vehicle, the defendant had pulled down his pants, rolled down his window, and stuck his bare backside and genitals out for them to see.

"I could tell that the defendant was agitated about the Crown's version of events, so I asked him if he had anything to say about the incident.

"'I certainly do, Your Honor,' the young man said, indignantly. 'It didn't happen like they say.'

"'Oh?' I asked, and the defendant replied: 'No! I didn't roll the window down!'"

In a trial that took place in 1984 in Kamloops, British Columbia, before County Court Judge George W. Lamperson, a man named Parish pleaded not guilty to a charge of obtaining video equipment while using someone else's identification. It was alleged that he used the I.D. of a man whose surname was Quechuk.

The Crown Attorney attempted to call a Mr. Quechuk as a witness for the prosecution, but things went wrong from the start. Mr. Quechuk, who'd been brought from the penitentiary to testify, had just entered the witness box when all hell broke loose. Here's the dialogue:

COURT CLERK: Take the Bible in your right hand. Do you swear that —
WITNESS: I don't believe in that stuff.
CLERK: Do you wish to affirm?
WITNESS: What is that?
CLERK: Do you solemnly affirm —
WITNESS: Sure, I guess.
CLERK: — that the evidence you give —
WITNESS: I do, I guess.
CLERK: Do you solemnly swear —
WITNESS: I guess so.
JUDGE: I'm not sure that the witness was sworn in.
WITNESS: Be right point blank, I don't got fuck all to say and as far as I can say you can take this fucking courtroom and shove it up your ass.
JUDGE: Take him away and I'll decide what to do with him.
WITNESS: Blow it out your asshole, you goat!

Later, Judge Lamperson dismissed the charges against the accused, Parish, and sentenced Quechuk to thirty days in jail for his naughty language and contempt of court. He was already serving four years at the time.

Quechuk insisted that he'd been misquoted. He wanted to set the record straight.

"Your Honor," he protested, "I did not call you a 'goat.' What I said was, 'Blow it out your asshole, you *goof.*'"

In 1979, in Toronto, a man pleaded guilty to a charge of bestiality and, as is the custom when there's a guilty plea, the Crown Attorney told the judge the basic facts of the case.

Toronto lawyer John P. Moise, Q.C., did not act as counsel for the defense, but, legal scholar that he is, he secured a transcript of what was said in court. Jack kindly supplied me with a copy of this brief document and I thought it would be downright unfair to deprive hordes of depraved citizens of the opportunity to give this gem a gander. So here it is:

CROWN ATTORNEY: On December 13th, last year, the accused apparently didn't have a home and he was invited to stay at a home operated by the Christian Fellowship Organization.

In the early morning hours of December 21st, his roommate awoke and observed the accused having an act of sexual intercourse with a dog that was present in the room. This dog was an Irish setter, about a year and a half old.

ACCUSED: Excuse me, sir. It wasn't an Irish setter. It was an *English* setter.

In an Iowa courtroom, a man charged with a felony — a serious crime — took the stand in his own defense. The prosecutor had the defendant's criminal record in his hand and he began to question him about it, hoping he'd deny some or all of it and so seal his own doom.

"Have you ever been convicted of a felony?" he asked.

"Yes."

"How many times?"

Realizing that the jig was up, the defendant replied: "This will make it four."

Jack Hughes, Criminal Trial Coordinator at the Toronto Courthouse, recalls a case in which the accused had such a long record that he could well expect to be parked away for three or four years.

The Crown Attorney started reading the record to the judge, but His Honor nodded off about twenty seconds into the recitation. He came to just as the prosecutor was finishing.

Hughes files this pithy report:

"The judge blinked and said, 'From what I've just heard, I'd say you deserve thirty days in jail.'

"The accused jumped up and said, 'I'll *take* it! I'll *take* it!'

"And he did."

Toronto lawyer Michael T. Wadsworth, Q.C., files an eyewitness report. One morning in the early 1970s, Wadsworth was sitting in a Toronto courtroom, waiting for his case to be called, when a chipper young man was brought before Provincial Court Judge Sidney R. Roebuck. He was charged with theft under fifty dollars.

As the accused looked around the room, smiling at everyone, the Crown Attorney announced that he wanted a detention order, even though the charge was minor. He said he hadn't had an opportunity to look into the man's background and the investigating officer wasn't available to assist him in that regard. Also, the accused hadn't yet spoken to counsel.

"Young man, do you understand what's happening here?" Judge Roebuck asked the prisoner at the bar. "The Crown Attorney is seeking a detention order against you. He wants to keep you in custody until your trial. Do you understand that?"

"Yeah, I understands," the fellow said, grinning.

"Well, you'll have to tell me something about yourself," the judge continued. "Where are you from?"

"St. John's, Newfoundland, Me Honor. I'm up here looking for work."

"Where do you live?"

"I live wit me brudder."

"Where does he live?"

"Me brudder lives wit me."

"But where?"

"Bloor Street — somewheres on Bloor Street."

"Well, I'm going to put your case over until this afternoon so the Crown can find out whether you've been in trouble with the law before."

"Oh, well, I'll tell ya. I've got twenty-two charges against me back in Newfoundland."

"Twenty-two charges!" His Honor exclaimed.

"Yeah, for car teft. But it's all the same car — me cousin's car. I stole it twenty-two times."

"Well, young man," said the judge, "you're in a *great deal* of trouble!"

"Why d'ya say dat, Me Honor? Dey hasn't *caught* me yet!"

Toronto lawyer Douglas C. Woolley, Q.C., tells a tale about the legendary Ottawa Valley magistrate, William K. ("Willie") MacGregor. His Worship, a man of prodigious thirst, was known far and wide as an extremely lenient sentencer — especially when grog was involved. As he liked to say, outside of court, "Man can't live by bread alone."

One day, back in the 1950s, MacGregor fined a woman a paltry twenty dollars for bootlegging. In a flash, she fished the fine from her bosom and quipped: "Aha, Willie, I bet you thought there were only tits down there!"

George R. Houlding, Q.C., a well-known counsel in Brantford, Ontario, reminisces about a fellow who appeared in court regularly in that city on charges of being intoxicated in a public place.

"He usually got terribly drunk on cheap wine," George wrote, "but one particular day he seemed to be in far better spirits. He pleaded guilty to the charge and Judge John T. Shillington, a kindly gentleman, looked at him and said, 'Well, Tom, wine again?'"

"Then came the unsolicited commercial. The accused looked at the judge from the dock and a smile broke out on his face and he replied, 'No, Captain,' which he always called the judge, 'nothing but the best — Teacher's Highland Cream!'

"This brought down the house and Judge Shillington gave him about half the usual sentence."

Former Provincial Court Judge S. Tupper Bigelow also had extensive experience in military law.

"In the late 1940s," he told me, "I presided over a court-martial in Winnipeg where an airwoman was charged with theft of a ring from a comrade. So far as I am aware, this was the first time a woman Air Force officer had ever been charged in a court-martial in Canada.

"Defence counsel produced witnesses who stated that the ring described by the complainant was a common or 'garden-variety' ring. They said there were probably hundreds of rings that matched the description of the complainant's ring.

"On the basis of defense counsel's argument, and the evidence of a jeweler called as an expert witness, I told the accused I was dismissing the charge against her.

"She then asked if she could ask a question and I told her she could, whereupon she said: 'Do I have to give the ring back to the woman I stole it from?'"

In Newfoundland, as everywhere else, folks like to visit friends and relatives at Christmastime. They do all the standard, traditional things — exchange presents, hoist a few "jars," swap some yarns, catch up on the latest news and gossip — and rarely does anything untoward occur.

One Yuletide, however, in one of the outports, a dastardly and unprecedented crime took place. Shortly after a certain reveler left one of the homes in the village, it was discovered that a Christmas gift, a Newfoundland tartan shirt, was missing from under the tree.

The suspect was approached by family members, but he firmly denied that he'd copped the shirt. The alleged culprit was charged with theft and the local magistrate heard the case.

Most of the evidence was circumstantial and the magistrate concluded that the prosecution had not proven guilt beyond a reasonable doubt. He told the accused he was acquitted.

"'Acquitted,' Me Honor?" asked the former accused. "Does that mean I can wear the shirt now?"

Toronto lawyer Alfred M. Kwinter once represented a break-and-enter artist who was charged with pulling more than a hundred jobs in a ritzy part of town.

"My client was a real pro," Alf reports. "He had a notebook in which he kept detailed records of all the things he stole — and the places he stole them from. When he was caught he decided to make a clean breast of everything and he showed his notes to the police.

"They compared this information with what various property-owners had reported stolen, and it was obvious that a lot of inflated insurance claims had been submitted. The accused exposed many of these people.

"From time to time during the trial my client would consult his notebook and interrupt a witness with such comments as, 'Not true, Your Honor! and 'No carpets were taken in *that* apartment!' My God, it seemed that my client, a professional thief, was the only honest guy in the room!"

Provincial Court Judge C. Emerson Perkins of Chatham, Ontario, writes:

"In a reminiscing conversation with Henry R. Howitt, former criminal court judge in Guelph, he told me a story that took place in London, Ontario.

"A man charged with assault appeared for trial without counsel before Magistrate D. B. Menzies. He claimed self-defense and went into the witness box to establish his claim. The dialogue went as follows:

ACCUSED: Sure I hit him, Your Worship, but he had a knife behind his back while he tried to provoke a fight.
MAGISTRATE: How did you know he had a knife?
ACCUSED: I just knew.
MAGISTRATE: Did you *see* the knife?
ACCUSED: No.
MAGISTRATE: If you didn't see the knife, how did you know he had one?
ACCUSED: Well, Your Worship, I ain't never seen it, but I *know* I've got an asshole.

Folks can get pretty confused by some of the lingo used in court. Vancouver lawyer David Griffiths sent me a transcript of the opening moments of a preliminary inquiry held recently in his city on a charge of robbery:

JUDGE: You have the option to elect to be tried by a Provincial Court judge without a jury and without having had a preliminary inquiry, or you may elect to have a pre-liminary inquiry and to be tried by a judge without a jury, or you may elect to have a preliminary inquiry and to be tried by a court composed of a judge and jury. How do you elect to be tried?

ACCUSED: I'd like preliminary without judge and jury — without the judge, anyway.

When an accused person has made a statement to police while being questioned about his possible involvement in a crime, the trial judge must be satisfied that whatever the accused said was said voluntarily and was not the product of fear, threat, or inducement. If the situation is otherwise, the words spoken cannot form part of the evidence at the trial.

A "trial within a trial" is held to determine whether the confession or other statement was, in fact, made voluntarily. Spectators, expecting to hear something "juicy," often lean on every word during this part of the festivities.

Mr. Justice George L. Murray of the Supreme Court of British Columbia sent me a transcript of part of a "trial within a trial" in an attempted-murder case. It has to do with the testimony of a police officer, and here's how it goes:

A. I advised him at that point that I was a peace officer and I advised that "it is my duty as a peace officer to instruct you that you have the right to seek and retain legal counsel without delay." I subsequently informed him that he was not obliged to say anything and anything he did say could be used in evidence against him, and the accused made a response to that at that time.

Q. He responded?

A. Yes, he did, Your Honor.

Q. And what did he say to that?

A. I asked him if he understood what I told him. He replied, "I understand what you're telling me and I only have one thing to say — fuck you."

D. G. Pahl, a Justice of the Peace in Thunder Bay, Ontario, sends this titillating tale:

"A now-deceased inspector of the Ontario Provincial Police told me this story. While he was stationed in the Manitoulin area, an exceptionally handsome native man was charged with rape. During his trial, the courtroom was packed with local women, many of them married.

"The defendant chose to give evidence and, during his examination in chief, his counsel, pointing to the victim, asked, 'Did you have intercourse with this woman?'

"The defendant stared at him, blankly. Counsel tried again: 'Did you have sexual relations with this woman?' Another blank look.

"Counsel then turned to His Lordship and explained that his client was a very unsophisticated person and that he would have to rephrase his question in the plainest terms.

"Again, turning to his client and pointing to the victim, he asked, 'Did you fuck this woman?'

"The defendant replied, 'No, I didn't.' And then, pointing to various females in the audience, he said, 'But I fucked her . . . and her . . . and her . . . and her.'

"In no time at all, the courtroom practically emptied."

Provincial Court Judge P. C. Marshall of Edmonton recently received a letter from a man he'd convicted and fined. The man wanted an extension of time to pay the fine.

"The information was attached to the letter," Judge Marshall says. "It showed that a month before I had fined the accused $100 for theft of condoms from a local drugstore. I had given him a month to pay the fine.

"On the form used when requesting an extension of time to pay a fine, under the words 'reason for request,' the accused had written, 'My wife got pregnant.'"

Toronto lawyer Robert B. McGee, Q.C., checks in with a touching tale from the front.

One day in the late 1980s, a Toronto lawyer, who shall remain nameless, represented a man on a fairly minor criminal charge before a Toronto judge who shall also remain nameless. The judge had served overseas in World War II and was justly proud of his contribution to the defense of international freedom.

After entering a guilty plea on behalf of his client, counsel made a short pitch which went pretty much as follows: "My client is sixty-nine years old, married and employed. He's never been in trouble before, Your Honor, and he served his country valiantly in

Africa, Italy, and on the beaches at Normandy. He was wounded on D-Day and was decorated for valor in the field."

Then the lawyer sat down.

The judge, noting the defendant's "excellent" war record, decorated him again — with an absolute discharge.

At the sound of the verdict, the defendant jumped up, and in a deep, guttural voice exclaimed: "*Danke schön!*"

John Jamieson, of Wingham, Ontario, is a retired Toronto policeman. He likes to reminisce about the good old days on the Accident Squad — especially when it comes to the story that follows.

Once he and fellow officers were called to an accident where a car hit a train at a level crossing controlled by a 'wig-wag' system. The driver wasn't injured, though he had hit the side of the engine. After their investigation, they charged him with careless driving. He pleaded not guilty.

When all the evidence had been presented in court, the magistrate asked the accused some questions about the accident:

"Didn't you see the train?"

"No, Your Worship, the sun was in my eyes and it blinded me."

"Didn't you see the wig-wag?"

"No, like I say, I was blinded by the sun."

"When the wig-wag is going, there's a bell that clangs very loudly. Didn't you hear that?"

"No, I didn't, sir."

"Why not?"

"Because of all the noise from the train whistle."

15

IMAGINATION

A MAN WITHOUT IMAGINATION IS LIKE A BIRD WITHOUT WINGS.

Wilhelm Raabe

IMAGINATION IS MORE IMPORTANT THAN KNOWLEDGE.

Albert Einstein

Imagination can be found in great abundance in our courts. Indeed, there are times when you'll encounter more flights of fancy in a court of law than you would at Disneyland. Ingenious and inventive lawyers are the chief culprits, but accused persons, litigants, and witnesses have their innings, too.

Let's nip into court and peruse a pile of incriminating evidence.

"There's no better way of exercising the imagination than the study of law," an observer of the legal scene once noted. "No poet ever interpreted nature as freely as a lawyer interprets truth."

Provincial Court Judge P.C. Marshall of Edmonton provides an introduction to that very kind of lawyer.

"I recently found a young man guilty of theft after a fairly lengthy trial," Judge Marshall writes. "In speaking to sentence, defense counsel was very eloquent.

"'You see that young lady in court, Your Honor,' he said. 'She's been here throughout the trial.'

"He then explained that she and the accused had formed 'a

beautiful relationship' and since that time the accused had 'completely turned his life around' and now he was going to become a great man. His future prospects were now virtually unlimited. Such a relationship was of Divine origin, and, it was submitted, the magnificent destiny that now lay ahead for this reformed young man should not be lightly interfered with.

"'Please do not destroy it all by sending him to jail,' the lawyer pleaded.

"With heavy heart, I informed counsel that since this was the fourth similar offense committed by the accused I must send him to jail for thirty days. I then left the courtroom and later the court clerk told me what transpired as soon as I'd gone.

"The young lady said to the accused, 'Give me a call when you get out,' and the accused replied: 'I sure will. By the way, sweetie, what's your last name?'"

Mr. Justice Willard ("Bud") Estey of the Supreme Court of Canada once asked an over-imaginative counsel: "Are you slicing the meat so thin because you hope it won't look like baloney?"

As a jurist of long standing, His Lordship well knew that from time to time judges are invited to dine on indigestible baloney. And as I hope to prove — beyond a reasonable doubt — it ain't always sliced so thin.

Judge Anthony Falzetta, of Sudbury, Ontario, presided at a trial that must have made him feel he was back in Sixth Grade.

The accused was charged with refusing to take a breathalyzer test. When asked to do so, he replied: "I ain't taking no goddamn breath test!"

Counsel for the defense argued that his client had used a double negative, which everybody — even judges — knows is "the same as a positive." In effect, he contended, the accused had said that he *would* take the test — and it wasn't his fault if the police didn't take him up on it.

Nice try, but no cigar.

Crown Attorney Brian Farmer tells about a "refuse to blow" case he prosecuted in Walkerton, Ontario.

The accused, an elderly man equipped with dentures, testified that he'd been having a devil of a time trying to keep his choppers from sliding around in his mouth. He solved the problem, he said, by anchoring his plate in place with Krazy Glue.

That was the good news.

The bad news was that the glue was so effective he couldn't open his mouth to blow into the breathalyzer machine.

"I didn't *refuse* to blow, Your Honor," said the accused. "I *couldn't* blow."

Judge F. W. Olmstead thought there was something Krazy about this defense and found the man guilty as charged.

Canada no longer has any "lay" magistrates — jurists totally lacking in formal legal education — but they used to abound. Many a lawyer wishes they'd never been phased out (a process that began in the 1960s) because it was easier to bamboozle such adjudicators than "the regular kind."

In a case heard thirty years ago by a lay magistrate, a Winnipeg lawyer represented a man who was charged with "leaving the scene of an accident." When the Crown's evidence had been presented, learned defense counsel rose to his feet and declared that the charge should be tossed out, forthwith.

"Your Worship," he said, "you've heard some evidence that shows that my client deliberately caused the mishap."

"Yes," said the magistrate, "but so what?"

"Well, it's really quite logical, sir," replied the lawyer. "If the incident in question was caused deliberately, then it wasn't an 'accident' and so it follows — just as surely as night follows day — that my client can't possibly be guilty of leaving the scene of an 'accident' because there *wasn't* any accident."

"I see what you mean," said His Worship. "There'll be an acquittal."

Provincial Court Judge C. C. Barnett of Williams Lake, British Columbia, has proof positive that such shenanigans as the foregoing are still practiced in court — sometimes even by law students.

"In 1976," His Honor reports, "I presided at the trial of a young fellow who was charged with having been a minor in licenced premises. He was defended by an articling law student.

"Crown Counsel called the accused's mother to the stand to prove that her son was under nineteen years of age at the time he was found in a pub. The law student objected to her testimony, stating that it was hearsay. His 'reasoning' was that since the mother had been anesthetized in the delivery room she had not actually witnessed the birth of her son and therefore it was possible that a mix-up had occurred and the accused was 'not really her son.'

"Happily, I understand that counsel's career at the bar was short."

Provincial Court Judge James Fontana of Ottawa reminisces about a client he represented when he was practicing law.

"A young, not-too-swift fellow was charged with a minor criminal offense and had been released on a 'Promise to Appear.' I showed up in court on the appointed day but the client did not show and he couldn't be located.

"The judge issued a bench warrant for his arrest and three months later we were all in court again on the original charge, plus an additional charge of failing to attend court when required to do so.

"The judge convicted my client on the original charge but dismissed the count of failure to attend court and had some difficulty suppressing his laughter. The client's explanation was: 'They made me sign that there Promise to Disappear, so I done the right thing and went out west for a few months.'"

Toronto lawyer John P. Moise, Q.C., recalls the case of a young lady who didn't get the benefit of the doubt when facing a charge of failing to appear in court.

"I rode my bike down to the court at Old City Hall," she told the judge, "but when I got there I saw a sign on the big outside door that said, 'No Peddlars.' So I went home."

Lawyers often have to be daring in their arguments, but, really, some counsel have more nerve than Dick Tracy.

In 1980, a Winnpeg lawyer defended a man on charges of rape and assault causing bodily harm. After a trial in which the complainant alleged that not only had she been raped by the accused but had also been severely beaten by him, a conviction was registered on each charge.

Addressing the court on the matter of sentence, the lawyer noted that his client was now living with a second common-law wife, having divorced his legal wife and ended a previous common-law relationship. He said his client "has shown that he is capable of forming close, satisfying emotional relationships with people — with women in particular."

When making a pitch to a court, it sometimes helps if a lawyer can say that his client is married — or is at least on the verge of committing matrimony. Sandra Spicer, a court reporter in Grande Prairie, Alberta, recently preserved the remarks of a lawyer who had nothing to go on but a smidgen of optimism:

"Your Honor," he said, "the accused has no girlfriend but he advises me that he is giving consideration to the possibility of marrying this summer or this fall."

Lawyers require nimble minds that enable them to switch gears rapidly. Donald F. McCrimmon, a lawyer in Medicine Hat, Alberta, tells of a fast-thinking colleague:

"Roger Jensen, a resourceful Medicine Hat criminal lawyer, appeared as duty counsel in Criminal Docket Court. He was required to act on behalf of a transient who had been charged with a number of offenses involving worthless checks for such things as motor vehicles and lodging.

"After a very short interview, it was time to go ahead with the bail hearing. When the Crown Prosecutor stood up to recite the previous convictions, Roger heard for the first time a lengthy litany, stretching back some twelve years, which included sixty-three bad check (false pretenses) convictions, fifteen fraud convictions, ten assorted thefts, procuring for the purposes of prostitution and — slipped in amongst the others — one conviction for failure to appear.

"The reading of this extensive list took a considerable amount of time and, during it, Roger somehow missed the failure-to-appear conviction.

"When asked what he had to say on the accused's behalf, Roger said that although his client had an extremely extensive record and no means of support or fixed place of abode, he had never failed to appear for court before.

"The judge corrected him, saying that his notes indicated one failure-to-appear conviction. The Crown Prosecutor agreed.

"Roger, thinking quickly, took a moment to reflect, then stated on his client's behalf: 'Yes, Your Honor, but it's very small considering the number of times he *could* have failed to appear.'"

Colin D. McKinnon, Q.C., of Ottawa, loves to tell the story of a fellow he once prosecuted on a charge of indecent assault. The accused, a well-known local lush, had been found sitting on a curb with his head under the dress of a woman.

In court, the man represented himself. His "defense" was that it was a windy day, he had only one match left, and he thought that the woman, who was "just sitting there anyway," wouldn't mind if he popped his head under her dress just long enough for him to light his cigarette.

"I was just getting ready to light up when the police grabbed me," said the accused, seconds before being sent to the slammer.

In 1970, a man represented himself in the Court of Appeal of British Columbia and argued with great vigor that he shouldn't have been convicted of murder a few months earlier. The Honorable N. T. Nemetz sent me a transcript of some interesting dialogue between himself and the appellant in the Court of Appeal:

MR. JUSTICE NEMETZ: Is it your point that this man Hall took the rifle out of your hands? You shot this man. There is no doubt about that, is there? Let us get down to the facts. You shot him?

APPELLANT: No, I did not.

MR. JUSTICE NEMETZ: You did not shoot him?

APPELLANT: No.

MR. JUSTICE NEMETZ: How did he get killed? Did lightning strike him?

APPELLANT: No. The best possible explanation, it was just that after the bullet expended, he just committed suicide.

Before he went on the bench, Mr. Justice George L. Murray of the Supreme Court of British Columbia argued many appeals on behalf of the Crown. One case concerned an ingenious fraud artist who duped hundreds of citizens into sending mounds of money to an organization of his own creation — to wit, "the Translation Army." Smart cookie that he was, the swindler knew that many folks would only glance at his impressive letterhead and assume they were remitting funds to the world-renowned Salvation Army.

In due course, the perpetrator was tried, convicted, and packed off to prison. A few days later, he filed a Notice of Appeal, also of his own creation, which stated that he should not have to serve time because that would "interfere with the good work of the Translation Army."

Norman Gulko of Toronto spent thirty-six years as a social worker with the Children's Aid Society. He wrote to me recently about a memorable court appearance made in the early 1960s by the mother of a child "apprehended" by the CAS when mama was accused of being a prostitute:

"One of our social workers went to court with the mother to be supportive. However, the woman knew how to handle herself. She pleaded not guilty and when her turn came to take the stand, the magistrate, not even looking up from his papers, asked, 'So, what's your story?' Whereupon, the accused stated, 'I was *buying* sex, Your Worship. I didn't get money. I *gave* it.'

"The magistrate put down his pen, looked up with interest, and said, 'Tell me about it.'

"The accused said she was a single parent and, because of

some bad experience in the past, she didn't want to get involved in a permanent relationship with a man. 'But every now and then,' she added, 'I get horny and need a man. So I pick up a man who appeals to me and pay him for looking after my needs.'

"The magistrate looked intently at the woman and said, 'I've heard hundreds of stories, but never one like yours. Now, I don't know whether your story is true or not, but I'm going to give you the benefit of the doubt for your originality. Case dismissed.'"

From Halifax, Provincial Court Judge Pat Curran reports on a recent case in which the accused tried to explain away every scrap of damning evidence:

"A man was charged with impaired driving as a result of a minor collision just outside one of the local drinking establishments. The investigating police officers testified that he exhibited the 'usual signs of impairment' — in spades!

"His speech was not merely slurred, but utterly unintelligible. His eyes were fiery red, not just bloodshot. He very nearly collapsed with every step he took. His breath smelled like one-hundred percent alcohol. Notwithstanding the absence of breath-alyzer readings, it seemed that the Crown had an overwhelming case.

"Then the accused was called to the stand, which he reached with great difficulty. As soon as he began to speak it became clear that he had the thickest Newfoundland accent I had ever heard, with an impediment to boot.

"He testified that he was a gyproc taper who had worked ten hours on the day in question and his eyes were always red from gyproc dust. He said he had a bad leg that had been operated on shortly before the alleged offense.

"On the evening in question, he said, his brother had asked him to use his (the brother's) truck to pick up his brother's wife at the drinking place. According to him, the accident had happened because of his unfamiliarity with the truck.

"At that point I could no longer restrain myself.

"'Don't tell me,' I said. 'Let me guess. You were moonlighting as a wine-tester that evening and that caused the smell of alcohol on your breath.'"

Mr. Justice Frank Maczko of the Supreme Court of British Columbia reminisces about another case in which explanations were in order:

"My former law partner, T. L. Robertson, was acting for a man charged with impaired driving, and the case for the prosecution was somewhat weak. The strongest evidence was that the accused's car was weaving on the highway.

"The police evidence was that there were two people in the car, the accused and his girlfriend. The accused's explanation for the weaving was that his girlfriend was playing with his penis.

"He was acquitted."

His Lordship also recollects a case in which he was defense counsel:

"In the early 1960s, I represented a fellow who was charged with 'impaired navigation.' He'd been at a party, and after the party was over he headed home on his fishing boat. The boat somehow caught fire and sank.

"The theory of the Crown was that the fisherman was drunk, ran the boat onto some rocks and purposely lit the fire so that he could collect the insurance. They had no evidence of arson, but if he were convicted of impaired navigation his insurance policy would be void.

"The main witness for the Crown was a man who'd been at the party and alleged that he saw the accused in a drunken state before he left for his boat. Coincidentally, this man was also the adjuster for the insurance company that insured the accused's boat.

"A young lady was called as a witness for the Crown, but she didn't come up with the right answers. The prosecution was successful in having her declared a hostile witness and proceeded to cross-examine her.

"She admitted that she'd refused to dance with the accused at the party, but was reluctant to say why. The prosecutor was convinced that her reason for refusing was because the accused was drunk.

"Eventually, the judge ordered the witness to answer the question and she finally admitted she'd refused to dance because the accused had 'a bulge in the front of his pants.'

"I argued that that was evidence which supported the proposition that the accused was *sober*, rather than drunk. The accused was acquitted."

Sometimes it's the judge whose imagination gets a workout.

Recalling his days as an Ottawa lawyer, Mr. Justice James B. Chadwick of the Supreme Court of Ontario tells of an impaired-driving case he defended back in the 1960s, before breathalyzer tests were mandatory.

Chadwick's client was taken into custody about four o'clock one morning after a police officer saw his car weaving on the highway. At a rural police station, the officer asked his prisoner to take a breathalyzer test. He declined and was promptly charged with impaired driving. For the next three hours or more, captor and captive played cribbage.

At the trial, which was held before a judge who was known for his unpredictability, Chadwick asked the arresting officer, "How many games of cribbage did you lose?"

"Most of them," the officer replied.

When he heard that, the judge asked Chadwick, "Have you got a motion you'd like to make?"

"Uh . . . uh . . . yes, Your Honor," the lawyer said, "I move for dismissal of the charge."

"Your Honor," said the Crown Attorney, "I have several witnesses I'd like to call."

"I don't have to hear from them," the judge replied. "The accused played crib with the policeman all night — and kept winning. He wasn't impaired. Case dismissed."

In the 1940s and '50s, before he was appointed to the Supreme Court of Ontario, the Honorable Leo Albert Landreville had an ideal client. He was Joseph Laflamme, a handsome six-foot-two, 220-pound fellow who was always getting in trouble in and around the northern Ontario village of Gogama.

"Over a ten-year period I defended Joe Laflamme nearly every month — and he won every case!" says Landreville, who these days is counsel to a well-known Ottawa law firm.

"Joe always followed the same routine. He'd call me at my office in Sudbury and tell me what he was charged with, and the court date, but nothing more. He'd meet me at the train and as we walked to court I'd try to find out the facts of the case, but he'd never tell me. He'd say, 'In court, just ax me my name and where I live and I'll tell my story.' That was all the preparation I ever had."

Laflamme was a lawyer's dream — a client who came up with a winning defense and did 90 percent of the work to boot. In a criminal court, the accused beats the rap if, after the evidence has been presented, there's a "reasonable doubt" as to his guilt. Joe Laflamme would have made a tremendous lawyer, for he knew instinctively how to scare up a reasonable doubt.

The dynamic duo of Laflamme and Landreville first teamed up in 1947, when Joe was charged with illegally selling liquor. The local cop had spied a bulge in the jacket of one Louis Labine and, suspecting that the bulge contained booze, had demanded that Labine reveal what he was lugging around with him. The officer was right, and the sealed bottle of rye whiskey thus intercepted became Exhibit 1 at the trial of Joe Laflamme.

In court, in the basement of the Catholic church, an overflow crowd heard the policeman testify that he'd asked Labine where he got the bottle and was told, "I got it from Joe Laflamme for ten dollars." Landreville had no cross-examination.

The next witness was Louis Labine.

"You heard the constable's testimony," the Crown Attorney said.

"Yes."

"Is this the man who sold you the bottle of liquor?" the prosecutor asked, pointing to Joe Laflamme.

"Yes."

"Is there anything you wish to add?"

"No," said Labine, with a trace of hesitation.

"That's the case for the Crown," the prosecutor said, somewhat triumphantly.

"I call Joseph Laflamme to the stand," Landreville announced.

After his client had been sworn in, the lawyer elicited his name and address and then said, "Now, you've heard what the constable and Mr. Labine have said under oath. What is your answer?"

"When I swear to tell the troot, I tell the troot!" Laflamme said for openers. "What they said is correct, but it's only part of the story. The officer never axed me before about this and I tell him now the whole story."

Laflamme then pointed to Louis Labine, in the front row, and said, "Labine, look here, if I tell a lie, stop me and say 'No!' — understand?"

Labine nodded. The magistrate and the lawyers were surprised at this tactic.

"Your Worship," the witness continued, "on that morning Labine come to my home. He said he has big head because of last night and he ax me if I got any liquor for sale. I tell him, *No!* That's because I'm on the blacklist at the Liquor Board.

"Now, Labine, remember I brought you to the balcony of my home and I pointed to the alley and a pile of wood in the backyard of the house that's two doors up the alley?"

Labine nodded.

"And, remember, I said, 'Go there and pull out third piece of wood from the end, on ground, put your arm in and you'll get a bottle of whiskey?'"

Labine nodded again.

"Then I said, 'Labine, for that *information* you pay me ten dollars.' And you gave me ten dollars, correct? Stand up, Labine, and tell the judge if that's true!"

Labine sprang from his seat and shouted, "Yes, that's true!"

Landreville had one more question: "You say that's exactly what happened, Mr. Laflamme?"

"Yes, for sure," the witness replied.

In his address to the magistrate, Landreville argued that there was no evidence to show that the accused owned the bottle of whiskey, and he pointed out that at no time was the hooch on his client's property or in his physical possession.

"Your Worship," he concluded, "there is a total lack of evidence in this case of the sale of liquor — only the sale of *information* as to where liquor could be found."

The magistrate then uttered two magic words: "Case dismissed."

The Honorable Allan McEachern, Chief Justice of the Supreme Court of British Columbia, speaks warmly of a former Vancouver magistrate:

"Mr. Gordon Scott was one of the finest and most human jurists ever to grace a bench in this province, or in any province. He had a rare sense of humor and a deep sense of forgiveness.

"He heard so many cases that he was always looking for something new, and it was said of Mr. Scott that any novel defense would gain an acquittal.

"One day, a large black gentleman was before Mr. Scott, charged with being in a state of intoxication in a public place.

"'What have you to say?' Mr. Scott inquired.

"'Well, Your Majesty,' replied the poor accused, 'it was St. Patrick's Day and I had a terrible case of pyorrhea of the central bicuspid and I just needed a drink to ease the awful pain, and...'

"'Say no more, my good man,' said Mr. Scott, 'Pyorrhea of the central bicuspid on St. Patrick's Day is a truly terrible affliction. The case is dismissed.'"

An informant who shall remain nameless files this report on an Alberta lawyer we'll call Jones:

"Mr. Jones was appointed by Legal Aid to defend a fellow who had 'borrowed' a car to drive home. He was apprehended along the way and charged with theft of a motor vehicle. A guilty plea was entered and, since the accused had a lengthy record for car theft, the Crown asked for a jail sentence.

"Defense counsel began his address to the court by pointing out that the accused, unlike the judge and lawyers, did not own a motor vehicle and was not polluting the atmosphere in the manner of other parties. He then launched into a lengthy address regarding the widespread pollution afflicting Canada and the dangers it represented to our society.

"When Mr. Jones had spoken only two or three sentences on that theme, the judge interrupted him to ask whether he was seriously suggesting that the accused should receive a lesser sentence because he wasn't polluting the atmosphere by operating a motor vehicle.

"Without the slightest hesitation, Mr. Jones replied that the court should certainly take such a factor into consideration. He then continued for a further ten minutes to decry the evils of pollution. When he was finished with that subject, he smoothly and quickly launched into the problems of overpopulation and the attendant dangers it represented to society.

"Mr. Jones advised the court that he was a member of an organization known as 'Zero Population Growth,' whose aim was to properly control the population of the earth to allow a full share of the resources to each individual. He then pointed out at some length the necessity of birth control.

"In the midst of his address, Mr. Jones suddenly turned to his client, who was meekly sitting in the prisoner's box with no apparent reaction to the remarks of his counsel, and asked him: 'Would you be willing to have a vasectomy to support Zero Population Growth and ensure that you did your part to stabilize the world's population?'

"His client did not respond but merely returned Mr. Jones's imploring look without any reaction. The lawyer continued his lecture and after a few more minutes sat down.

"The judge made no comment in his judgment but treated the matter as a routine case of an offender with a record and imposed a sentence of nine months in jail."

"There are no new defenses in the criminal law — only endless machinations of old ones," Edmonton lawyer W. J. Shortreed, Q.C., once observed.

Oh, I don't know about that! Weird and wonderful new defenses keep popping up with such refreshing regularity that, obviously, one hell of a lot of creative thinking is going on. Take drug cases, for example.

Judge C. C. Barnett, of Williams Lake, British Columbia, says that for sheer ingenuity the very best story he's heard was concocted in 1985 by a man he convicted on a charge of growing marijuana. He prefers not to name the accused, so he identifies him only by his initials — R.S.M. Take it away, Your Honor:

"R.S.M. was a strange man but a true genius at hay-wire mechanicking. He had a shed at his place which look like a mere chicken coop. In fact, it was all insulated, heated, and lighted, and many marijuana plants were happily growing inside, away from sight of prying eyes. He had put the whole thing together himself, using a variety of parts discarded by others as junk.

"When he testified, he told me that he was certainly not intending to sell or smoke an illegal substance. He told me that he had long been troubled by the plight of Western farmers who were all going broke growing cereal crops. He had heard about the remarkable plant which would grow almost anywhere and could be used to make rope and, he surmised, paper.

"R.S.M. claimed that his strain of marijuana plants grow wild in northern Russia and that he was doing scientific work attempting to lower the tetrahydrocannabinol (THC) content of the plants — the chemical that makes marijuana addictive — with each succeeding generation. He explained that when he developed a strain of marijuana plants with a negligible THC content, he would approach the federal government to have it legalized. And he added that he believed that this new crop would be the salvation of prairie farmers in Canada.

"Scout's honor, that's what the man said."

Judge Barnett remembers another far-fetched defense:
"I recall a 'back-to-the-land' type who appeared before me charged with possession of marijuana for the purpose of trafficking. The police had found a pound or so of the stuff in his home, in a remote area near Williams Lake.

"The man appeared without counsel and testified that he had heard that people who smoke marijuana tended to gain weight. So, he said, he had acquired some marijuana to feed to his cow, along with good alfalfa hay, to see if he could fatten her up more quickly.

"Crown Counsel thought it was a good story and agreed to reduce the charge to one of simple possession."

Here's the verbatim account of some of the dialogue in a case heard in Toronto by Judge Robert B. Dnieper:

JUDGE: You're not a stranger to marijuana. You've used it.

ACCUSED: Yeah, I use it. . . . but I didn't have no marijuana in my house.

JUDGE: But you had the seeds.

ACCUSED: Yeah, but I give my bird marijuana seeds.

JUDGE: Oh, you've got a pretty healthy bird?

ACCUSED: Yeah, they love it. I got a canary.

JUDGE: You've got a canary. He must sing some pretty tunes, doesn't he? Have you ever laid a charge against a canary, counsel?

CROWN ATTORNEY: I don't believe so, Your Honor.

JUDGE: Defense, are you calling evidence from the canary?

COUNSEL: No.

JUDGE: I don't want to anticipate the net result, but maybe the canary will sing for us. . . . Counsel, do you want time to bring the bird in?

COUNSEL: No.

JUDGE: I'll give you all the time you like, counsel, because I haven't heard from a canary in a long time. . . . The accused admits he serves seeds to his bird. I don't know, I guess they should've charged both of them. I guess the police officers didn't realize that.

From now on, you have to be careful what you feed that bird. He's in trouble. There will be a search warrant to bring in the bird.

In 1980, Kingston, Ontario, lawyer Fergus J. O'Connor had a merry old time defending a client who was charged with possession of marijuana for the purpose of trafficking.

Evidence disclosed that O'Connor's client had stolen a coat from a store and escaped in a van driven by another man. A security guard who chased them in a car testified that he saw the passenger throw a garbage bag from the van as it sped through the streets of Kingston. The bag was recovered and found to be filled with marijuana. A short time later, police stopped the van and charged the occupants.

"My client had a notebook on him that contained the names of various persons and, beside each name, a reference to a number of ounces," O'Connor writes. "Also in the notebook was a recipe for that ever-popular Polish dish — perogies. My client was Polish.

"Part of my client's defense at trial was that the marijuana was locally grown and of poor quality and was for the personal use of the driver of the van. My client testified that he had no knowledge of its presence in the van until he and his co-accused were being chased after the theft of the coat.

"Regarding the notebook, the theory of the defense was that my client was a gourmet cook who made perogies for friends and acquaintances, and the entries in the book related to orders he had for perogies. Thus, we were pursuing the case as one of 'trafficking in perogies.'

"The co-accused took the stand and confirmed that he knew my client to be a gourmet cook, and further, that my client did not have knowledge of the presence of marijuana in the vehicle.

"Then, on the final day scheduled for presenting evidence to judge and jury, my client, presumably after weighing the evidence in his own mind, chose not to attend court. The judge ordered that the trial proceed in his absence.

"The only evidence I was able to call on behalf of my client was that of an expert in the making of perogies. He testified as to the quantities of ingredients needed to make that dish and this enabled me to argue that the numbers in the notebook were consistent with orders for perogies.

"In my address to the jury, I said: 'Ladies and gentlemen, I submit that this is a case of trafficking, not in marijuana, but perogies. I also submit that, now that my client has left me all alone to argue on his behalf, this case might well go down in history as "the case of the galloping gourmet."'

"The jury got a tremendous laugh out of my summation, but they found my client guilty and he was sentenced to twelve months in jail."

Judge H. Russell MacEwan of New Glasgow, Nova Scotia, reminisces as follows:
"In my first year on the bench I tried a charge of possession of

hashish. The Crown proved a small residue of 'hash' in a pipe that resembled a musical instrument.

"Following the Crown's case, the accused took the stand and said that he'd found the pipe on the street and kept it so he could play it in a local orchestra, of which he was a member.

"Being possessed of what I thought was a superior knowledge at the time, and to clarify the matter, I asked the accused if he could play a tune on the instrument. He seized same, placed it to his lips, and played in loud, clear notes the refrain 'Yankee Doodle Dandy.'

"I acquitted the accused of the charge, forthwith."

Judge James A. Fontana of Ottawa, a former Crown Attorney, recalls a case heard in his neck of the woods:

"Stories about Bob Barr, legendary Brockville lawyer, abound. He is bold and quick.

"One day Barr pleaded a client guilty to a charge of simple possession of cocaine and made a strong pitch for a discharge, despite the fact that Judge R. M. MacFarlane usually imposed a jail term for any cocaine-related offense.

"Judge MacFarlane looked at Barr incredulously, seeking some explanation for his out-of-the-ballpark request.

"'But it was just diet coke, Your Honor,' Barr quipped, to no avail except resounding laughter in the courtroom."

Sydney, Nova Scotia, lawyer David N. Muise sent me a newspaper article about a couple of Cape Breton men who, in January 1990, pleaded not guilty to charges of unlawfully attempting to hunt or kill wildlife at night.

Conservation officers testified that one night the previous fall they saw a light coming from the roof of a truck owned by one of the accused, whom I'll call Fraser. The headlights of the truck were also on, they said, and they found the co-accused, referred to herein as Cameron, hiding in the bush with a loaded rifle nearby. Cameron, court was told, is a butcher.

The accused men, who represented themselves at the trial, said they went to the woods that night, not to hunt, but to search for two sheep that had wandered away from Fraser's property.

Fraser told the court he knew he'd be breaking the law if he hunted at night, but he didn't think there was anything wrong with looking for lost sheep. He said he asked Cameron to help in the search and he added that if they found the sheep they were going to shoot them and Cameron would then butcher them.

Cameron testified that at one point he took the spotlight off the truck and climbed down a hill to see if the sheep were there. He said he then heard a commotion and when he realized it was conservation officers talking to Fraser he hid the rifle — and himself — because he knew it was unlawful to have the rifle uncased.

"I was asked to do a job and I thought I'd have half a sheep for a few good feeds," Cameron told Judge George R. LeVatte.

Alas, all he got was a conviction and a fine of two hundred dollars and costs. Ditto for Fraser.

My informant, David Muise, reports that the case put forward by the defense was immediately enshrined in Cape Breton legal lore and is known, and will be forever known, as "the Bo-Peep Defense."

Ottawa lawyer Colin D. McKinnon, Q.C., tells of an offbeat defense that cropped up in a courtroom in his city.

One day, several years ago, a man got up from his table in an Ottawa bar and walked into the washroom. He was followed very shortly by another man. Soon thereafter, the first fellow staggered out of the washroom with a knife sticking out of his back. The second man was charged with attempted murder.

In court, the accused said he "noticed" the knife and even tried to remove it from the man's back, but he knew nothing about how it got there or who the perpetrator was.

"So you're using the SODDI defense, are you?" the Crown Attorney asked the accused on cross-examination.

"I'm not familiar with that term," the man replied. "Do you mean 'Saudi,' as in 'Saudi Arabia?'"

"No," interjected the judge, "he means S-O-D-D-I — as in 'Some Other Dude Done It!'"

Beware! Lawyers who love to make silk purses out of sows' ears should stay clear of Provincial Court Judge Nick Friesen of Quesnel, British Columbia. On December 15, 1989, at Anahim Lake, B.C., Judge Friesen pulverized a highly technical lawyer from Kamloops with language that will endear him to every jurist in the land. Here is part of His Honor's pronouncement:

"In Anahim Lake, the residents use common sense, which they sometimes call horse sense.

"There are lots of horses in Anahim Lake. Yesterday we saw more horses than usual in this settlement. It was by-election day and our usual courtroom, which is this hall, was used as a polling place. Some people came by horseback, tied their horses to the front door, and voted.

"Some horses left piles of manure at the doorstep. They did not, however, bring it into the courtroom. Now that is horse sense!

"Lawyers from Kamloops have to travel at least six hours to get to Anahim Lake. Lawyers generally have a very active mind. They have lots of time to dream up exotic arguments when they travel that long.

"However, they should pause at the front door of our court and look down and contemplate those piles of manure and their arguments. Had that been done in this case, the lawyer might have been heard to say 'That's horse shit!' and have left his argument outside the courtroom, too."

"There are strange things done in the midnight sun . . ."

Bruce MacAdam, a lawyer in Golden, British Columbia, concludes festivities with a classic yarn from the Yukon. An old-time miner named Bill Scott related the tale to Bruce in the summer of 1982 when they worked together on a gold dredge, sixty-five miles east of Dawson City.

"Mr. Scott, now deceased, spent almost all his adult life mining in the creeks of the Yukon," Bruce says. "He told me he'd checked the story out with many other miners, who'd been around even longer than he had, and they all said the story was true. I dug into the matter quite a bit myself and everyone I spoke to said it was true."

Back around 1910, a lonely goldminer was brought to court in Dawson City, charged with bestiality. The Crown alleged that he'd had his way with a "jenny" — i.e., female — mule.

There were no legally trained magistrates in the Yukon in those primitive days, and so the man who was to sit in judgment of the prisoner at the bar had only scanty formal knowledge of criminal law. The same was true of the prosecutor, who was not a lawyer but a member of the Royal Canadian Mounted Police. There was no lawyer to assist the accused, either, so he had to face the music alone.

When the grisly details had all been presented in evidence, the magistrate glared at the accused and said: "I don't know how you could do such a disgusting thing! Before I sentence you, is there anything you wish to say for yourself?"

"I had to do it, sir," the man replied, unwittingly laying the foundation for what today would be called the defense of necessity.

"What do you mean, you *had* to do it?"

"Well, sir, you see, I'm built so big that no woman can take me."

"No, I *don't* see, but now that you've mentioned the matter, I feel that I *have* to see — your instrument, that is. It could have a bearing on the case."

"I can't show it here . . . in court," said the accused.

"No, of course not," His Worship replied. "You can show it to me in my office. The prosecutor should see it, too, because, after all, it's a matter of evidence. Court is adjourned and will reconvene after we've had a look at this evidence."

The accused and the prosecutor trooped backstage to the magistrate's office.

Two or three minutes later, the three men returned to their battle stations and the magistrate immediately announced: "Case dismissed!"

Then, as an afterthought, he added, "And give this man back his mule!"

P.S.

It seems hard to believe, but there are still zillions of funny, true legal stories "out there." That's fortunate, indeed, because people are still clamoring for them. There'll be another one of these productions — the good Lord willin' and if the crik don't rise!

But, remember, it can't happen unless my suppliers keep supplying. I don't dream up these yarns, you know. They're real-life tales, told, usually, by people who were on hand when laughter erupted.

So, come on, folks, let's have those true, humorous legal anecdotes — the sooner the better because you might forget to do it later. You can send me your stories, by letter or tape, at the address shown below. As before, the names of contributors will be published in the book, ensuring them of at least some of the recognition they so richly deserve. Send your stories to:

Peter V. MacDonald, Q.C.,
555 - 18th Ave., Hanover, Ontario, N4N 3B2.

Oh yes, and should anyone seize upon the excellent idea of having me tell these and other tales before a live audience, arrangements can be made through **Laura M. Ferrier & Associates Inc., 449 Soudan Ave., Toronto, Ontario, M4S 1X1; telephone (416) 440-0463; fax (416) 440-0960.**

CONTRIBUTORS

Robert B. Aaron, Toronto, Ontario
David Acri, London, Ontario
R. S. Adams, Vernon, British Columbia
J. Trevor Alexander, Victoria, British
Columbia
Anthony Allman, Moncton, New
Brunswick
Johanne Amonson, Edmonton, Alberta
Janet M. Henley Andrews, St. John's,
Newfoundland
Abe Anhang, Winnipeg, Manitoba
Denis Archambault, Prince George, British
Columbia
R. Y. Archibald, Victoria, British Columbia
Regina Arthur, Meaford, Ontario
Bertha Ayers, Whitehorse, Yukon Territory
Joyce Abchli, Whitehorse, Yukon Territory
K. M. Baird, London, Ontario
Jonathan B. Baker, Vancouver, British
Columbia
R. B. Banham, Newcastle, Ontario
Ernie Banks, Toronto, Ontario
Judge G. J. Barnable, Placentia,
Newfoundland
Judge C. C. Barnett, Williams Lake, British
Columbia
Robert A. Barr, Q.C., Brockville, Ontario
Fred W. Barry, Nanaimo, British Columbia
Dahn Batchelor, Rexdale, Ontario
Charles M. Bauer, Ottawa, Ontario
Reving Belanger, Brockville, Ontario
Judge Thomas Bell, Saint John, New
Brunswick
Pearl Benyk, Yellowknife, Northwest
Territories
Norman Bercovich, Regina, Saskatchewan
Mr. Justice Ronald L. Berger, Edmonton,
Alberta
Joseph J. Berry, Guelph, Ontario
Jacques L. Berthiaume, Hull, Quebec
S. Tupper Bigelow, Q.C., Toronto, Ontario
Kenneth C. Binks, Q.C., Ottawa, Ontario
Martha S. Binks, Toronto, Ontario
Jim Biss, Saskatoon, Saskatchewan

Peggy J. Blair, Edmonton, Alberta
R. Don Blakely, Prince George, British
Columbia
Robert V. Blakely, Vernon, British
Columbia
Gillian Boothroyd, Vancouver, British
Columbia
Judge J. M. Bordeleau, Ottawa, Ontario
Mary E. E. Boyce, Toronto, Ontario
Sondra L. Braid, Winnipeg, Manitoba
Garry K. Braund, Q.C., Toronto, Ontario
Audrey S. Brent, Saskatoon, Saskatchewan
David Brisbin, Emerson, Manitoba
Chris Brower, Edmonton, Alberta
Barry G. Browning, Victoria, British
Columbia
Brian A. Bruser, Yellowknife, Northwest
Territories
David G. Bryce, Toronto, Ontario
Patricia L. Buchholz, Annapolis Royal,
Nova Scotia
D. W. Burns, Ottawa, Ontario
Stuart A. Busse, Q.C., Biggar,
Saskatchewan
Judge Milton A. Cadsby, Toronto, Ontario
Paul Calarco, Toronto, Ontario
Robert H. Cameron, Port Coquitlam,
British Columbia
Judge Grant A. Campbell, Kitchener,
Ontario
James D. Campbell, Embrun, Ontario
Judge C. J. Cannon, Etobicoke, Ontario
Ronald Cantlie, Calgary, Alberta
William M. Carlyle, Q.C., Vancouver,
British Columbia
Elijah (Nick) Carter, Niagara-on-the-Lake,
Ontario
D. Kevin Carroll, Q.C., Barrie, Ontario
John Carten, Comox, British Columbia
Judy A. Caruso, Sault Ste. Marie, Ontario
Renzo Catana, Ottawa, Ontario
Denis Chadbourn, North Bay, Ontario
Mr. Justice James Chadwick, Toronto,
Ontario

David Cheifetz, Toronto, Ontario

Leo B. Chrzanowski, Edmonton, Alberta

Michael E. Cobb, Simcoe, Ontario

Michael Cochrane, Toronto, Ontario

Thomas Cole, Toronto, Ontario

Maggie Collins, Calgary, Alberta

Robert L. Colson, Toronto, Ontario

Donald M. Cooper. Q.C., Yellowknife, Northwest Territories

Kathryn Craig, Walkerton, Ontario

James C. Crawford, Q.C. Calgary, Alberta

Bruce Crockett, Toronto, Ontario

Judge Kenneth L. Crowell, Middleton, Nova Scotia

Judge Pat Curran, Bedford, Nova Scotia

Grant M. Currie, Saskatoon, Saskatchewan

Greg Currie, Scarborough, Ontario

David C. Day, Q.C., St. John's, Newfoundland

Gail Debenham, Edmonton, Alberta

Paul A. Demong, Regina, Saskatchewan

Joseph de Pencier, Ottawa, Ontario

Donald J. Dermody, Shaunavon, Saskatchewan

Philippe Desjardins, Ottawa, Ontario

Daniel Doheny, Q.C., Montreal, Quebec

Raymond Donohue, Sarnia, Ontario

John G. ("Jake") Dunlap, Q.C., Ottawa, Ontario

Rev. Paul Driscoll, Markdale, Ontario

Bruce Duncan, Toronto, Ontario

Keith Eaton, Q.C., Chester Basin, Nova Scotia

Jacqueline Elliott, Canberra, Australia

Henry P. Estlin, Parksville, British Columbia

Michael Fairney, Thornhill, Ontario

R. Jack Falkins, Saute Ste. Marie, Ontario

Brian R. Farmer, Walkerton, Ontario

Judge E. B. Fedak, Newmarket, Ontario

Mr. Justice Joseph B. Feehan, Edmonton, Alberta

Judge James P. Felstiner, Willowdale, Ontario

W. J. Festeryga, Hamilton, Ontario

Donald J. Finn, Minden, Ontario

Judge F. S. Fisher, Islington, Ontario

Stanley G. Fisher, Q.C., Toronto, Ontario

Rodney E. Follwell, Belleville, Ontario

Judge James A. Fontana, Ottawa, Ontario

Judge M. Paul Forestell, Cayuga, Ontario

Frank Fowler, Q.C., St. John's, Newfoundland

Ronald J. Fromstein, Ajax, Ontario

Mr. Justice Patrick Galligan, Toronto, Ontario

Steven C. Gaon, Toronto, Ontario

Anthony J. Gargrave, Vancouver, British Columbia

Sharon Gateley, Whitehorse, Yukon Territory

Adam W. Germain, Q.C., Fort McMurray, Alberta

Mr. Justice Paul Godin, Campbellton, New Brunswick

Clifford S. Goldfarb, Toronto, Ontario

Chief Justice Noel H. A. Goodrige, St. John's, Newfoundland

William H. Goodridge, St. John's, Newfoundland

Dorrine Goltz, Etobicoke, Ontario

Thomas J. Gorsky, Toronto, Ontario

Jamie Graham, Spruce Grove, Alberta

John F. Grant, Campbell River, British Columbia

Stephen M. Grant, Toronto, Ontario

Brian L. Graves, Comox, British Columbia

J. T. (Ted) Green, Toronto, Ontario

William T. Green, Q.C., Ottawa, Ontario

David Griffiths, Vancouver, British Columbia

Eric K. Grossman, Toronto, Ontario

Keith F. Groves, Calgary, Alberta

Angel Guerra, Don Mills, Ontario

R. H. Guile, Q.C., Vancouver, British Columbia

Norman Gulko, Willowdale, Ontario

Judge Harold Gyles, Winnipeg, Manitoba

Douglas G. Haig, Q.C., Barrie, Ontario

Mr. Justice Doane Hallett, Halifax, Nova Scotia

Mr. Justice Raymond J. Halley, St. John's, Newfoundland

Donald V. Hambling, Q.C. Meaford, Ontario

Judge Garrett A. Handrican, Grand Bank, Newfoundland

Edward Hanman, Victoria, British Columbia

Roger Harris, Halifax, Nova Scotia

Judge Sydney M. Harris, Toronto, Ontario
Bernard Harrison, St. Catharines, Ontario
George Hartsell, London, Ontario
J. A. Hendriksen, Delta, British Columbia
Frederick H. Herbert, Q.C., Vancouver,
  British Columbia
Richard J. Hobson, Waterloo, Ontario
Gordon J. Hoffman, Calgary, Alberta
Judge Derek T. Hogg, Toronto, Ontario
Shirley Hooper, Toronto, Ontario
John D. Hope, Nanaimo, British Columbia
Douglas Hopkinson, Southampton,
  Ontario
Mark Hornblower, Sarnia, Ontario
George R. Houlding, Q.C., Brantford,
  Ontario
Judge Edward J. Houston, Ottawa,
  Ontario
Chief Judge Harry W. How, Halifax, Nova
  Scotia
John L. Hughes, Toronto, Ontario
David H. Jack, Fergus, Ontario
W. R. Jack, Victoria, British Columbia
Robert Jacks, Q.C., Collingwood, Ontario
John Jamieson, Wingham, Ontario
R. Lorne Jamieson, Saskatoon,
  Saskatchewan
Ronald R. Jeffels, Richmond, British
  Columbia
Doreen Johnson, Orleans, Ontario
R. G. Johnson, Wiarton, Ontario
Robert T. Johnston, Q.C., Victoria, British
  Columbia
Alfred D. Kaiser, Beamsville, Ontario
Sean Kelly, Bracebridge, Ontario
Mr. Justice William Kelly, Halifax, Nova
  Scotia
Judge David Kent, Sarnia, Ontario
Marie Kennedy, Edmonton, Alberta
Joel A. Kerbel, Toronto, Ontario
Donald A. Kerr, Q.C., Halifax, Nova Scotia
Mary Kimball, Halifax, Nova Scotia
Dr. D. E. L. King, Hamilton, Ontario
Brian D. Kinnear, Orillia, Ontario
Gordon I. Kirke, Q.C., Toronto, Ontario
Rudy Kominek, Waterloo, Ontario
Irene Kowalchuk, Whitehorse, Yukon
  Territory
Mr. Justice Horace Krever, Toronto,
  Ontario

Mr. Justice Joseph J. Kryczka, Calgary,
  Alberta
Alfred M. Kwinter, Toronto, Ontario
Terence La Liberté, Vancouver, British
  Columbia
Hon. L. A. Landreville, Q.C., Ottawa,
  Ontario
David Lawrence, Toronto, Ontario
Bert Lerch, Neustadt, Ontario
Al Lever, Renfrew, Ontario
Paul E. Levy, Surrey, British Columbia
Robert O. Levin, Kelowna, British
  Columbia
H. M. Lewin, Toronto, Ontario
Don Lindal, Winnipeg, Manitoba
Mr. Justice Rodman E. Logan, Saint John,
  New Brunswick
Bernard Loomis, Vernon, British
  Columbia
Judge Spyros D. Loukidelis, Sudbury,
  Ontario
Daniel Lyon, Toronto, Ontario
Bruce MacAdam, Golden, British
  Columbia
Angus G. Macdonald, Edmonton, Alberta
Michael Anne MacDonald, Bracebridge,
  Ontario
Rosemary Macdonald, Calgary, Alberta
Judge H. R. MacEwan, New Glasgow, Nova
  Scotia
Roderick G. MacGregor, Toronto, Ontario
Charles W. MacIntosh, Q.C., Halifax, Nova
  Scotia
Ronald F. MacIsaac, Q.C., Victoria, British
  Columbia
Genevieve MacKenzie, Whitehorse, Yukon
  Territory
Rev. A. F. MacSween, Saanichton, British
  Columbia
Mr. Justice Frank Maczko, Vancouver,
  British Columbia
George A. Marron, Q.C., Toronto, Ontario
Weldon C. Matthews, Q.C., Halifax, Nova
  Scotia
Chief Justice Allan McEachern, Victoria,
  British Columbia
Ed McCarroll, Toronto, Ontario
Robert J. McCleave, Halifax, Nova Scotia
Mr. Justice John W. McClung, Edmonton,
  Alberta

Dennis G. McCrea, Vancouver, British Columbia

Donald F. McCrimmon, Medicine Hat, Alberta

William McDonald, Georgetown, Ontario

John McDowell, Toronto, Ontario

Robert B. McGee, Q.C., Toronto, Ontario

Gail McGilvray, London, Ontario

Jil McIntosh, Oshawa, Ontario

Robert D. McIntyre, Q.C., Brampton, Ontario

Alexander F. McKean, Lebret, Saskatchewan

Ian F. McKee, Halifax, Nova Scotia

Richard D. McLean, Q.C., Toronto, Ontario

Judge T. B. McMeekin, Calgary, Alberta

Richard McNally, Edmonton, Alberta

Sal Merenda, Toronto, Ontario

Irene Meyer, Regina, Saskatchewan

Mr. Justice Perry Meyer, Montreal, Quebec

Paul R. Meyers, Richmond, British Columbia

Maria Mihailovich, Hamilton, Ontario

Mr. Justice Tevie H. Miller, Edmonton, Alberta

John P. Moise, Q.C., Toronto, Ontario

Carl Morgan, Windsor, Ontario

Laura Lee Mountain, Assiniboia, Saskatchewan

David N. Muise, Sydney, Nova Scotia

Col. D. Brian Murphy, Ottawa, Ontario

Gary Murphy, Hamilton, Ontario

William G. Murphy, Q.C., Toronto, Ontario

Robert Murrant, Q.C., Halifax, Nova Scotia

Mr. Justice George L. Murray, Vancouver, British Columbia

Hon. N. T. Nemetz, Victoria, British Columbia

Thomas A. Newman, Q.C., Pickering, Ontario

Judge John R. Nichols, Digby, Nova Scotia

D. J. O'Byrne, Terrace, British Columbia

Fergus J. O'Connor, Kingston, Ontario

R. J. O'Gorman, Calgary, Alberta

Thomas G. O'Neil, Saint John, New Brunswick

Hugh O'Neill, Q.C., St. John's, Newfoundland

Mr. Justice Seamus B. O'Regan, Happy Valley/Goose Bay, Newfoundland

Russell J. Otter, Toronto, Ontario

Robert A. Otto, Hamilton, Ontario

D. G. Pahl, Thunder Bay, Ontario

J. D. Palmer, Calgary, Alberta

Judge Claude H. Paris, Toronto, Ontario

Paul Parlee, Stratford, Ontario

Roland Paskar, Mississauga, Ontario

Dr. James Paterson, Willowdale, Ontario

Laura Pennigton, Edmonton, Alberta

Judge C. Emerson Perkins, Chatham, Ontario

Judge Robert Perras, North Bay, Ontario

Richard A. Pharand, Q.C., Sudbury, Ontario

Kenneth I. Picov, Toronto, Ontario

Charles A. Pope, Ottawa, Ontario

Edward J. Posliff, Windsor, Ontario

Deirdre Pothecary, North Vancouver, British Columbia

G. B. Purdy, Q.C., Vancouver, British Columbia

D. James Ramsay, Kelowna, British Columbia

Bert Raphael, Q.C., Toronto, Ontario

Neil M. Raven, Deep River, Ontario

Judge James D. Reardon, Yarmouth, Nova Scotia

Richard A. Reimer, Petawawa, Ontario

Henry J. Reiner, Vancouver, British Columbia

Laurie Revesz, Toronto, Ontario

Rosemary Rideout, Halifax, Nova Scotia

Patricia Robbins, Victoria, British Columbia

Robert Robertson, Tara, Ontario

J. Stewart Robertson, Trenton, Ontario

Sidney R. Roebuck, Toronto, Ontario

Arthur W. MacLeod Rogers, Q.C., Victoria, British Columbia

Alexander S. Romanchuk, St. Albert, Alberta

W. James Hope-Ross, Calgary, Alberta

Theresa Roth, Toronto, Ontario

Judge Dwayne W. Rowe, Sidney, British Columbia

Jay Rumanek, Montreal, Quebec

Om P. Sachdeva, St. Catharines, Ontario

James H. Schaffer, Erin, Ontario

Douglas Schofield, Hamilton, Bermuda

Arthur Scholefield, Victoria, British
  Columbia
Fred L. Scott, Calgary, Alberta
Jill E. Scrutton, London, Ontario
Judge C. Scullion, Toronto, Ontario
Colm St. R. Seviour, St. John's,
  Newfoundland
Mr. Justice Melvin E. Shannon, Calgary,
  Alberta ·
Judge B. Barry Shapiro, Brampton,
  Ontario
Paul Shaw, Thornbury, Ontario
Robert A. L. Shour, Toronto, Ontario
Morris C. Shumiatcher, Q.C., Regina,
  Saskatchewan
Murray D. Silverberg, Toronto, Ontario
Sidney B. Simons, Victoria, British
  Columbia
R. K. Simpson, Simcoe, Ontario
J. A. Sissons, Niagara Falls, Ontario
Donald W. Skogstad, Nelson, British
  Columbia
Max Slapack, Q.C., Westmount, Quebec
Pauline Smart, Vancouver, British
  Columbia
Angela M. Smith, Etobicoke, Ontario
Geraldine Smith, Placentia,
  Newfoundland
Stan Smith, Scarborough, Ontario
Emanuel Sonnenschein, Saskatoon,
  Saskatchewan
Sandra Spicer, Grande Prairie, Alberta
P. J. Stallwood, Cayuga, Ontario
Margaret Stapley, Stouffville, Ontario
John G. Starzynski, Oshawa, Ontario
Leonard W. Stewart, Q.C., Mississauga,
  Ontario
Steve Stirling, Port Alberni, British
  Columbia
Christine Stone, Edmonton, Alberta
Judge Ray Stortini, Sault Ste. Marie,
  Ontario
Maxine L. Strain, Lethbridge, Alberta
Chief Judge Hazen Strange, Oromocto,
  New Brunswick
Siona V. Sullivan, St. Catharines, Ontario
Ian Sutherland, Lethbridge, Alberta
Thomas R. Swabey, Cornwall, Ontario

Anne Swanston, Toronto, Ontario
Debra J. Sweetman, Whitby, Ontario
Peter F. Thompson, Midland, Ontario
David Tilley, Q.C., Edmonton, Alberta
Judge Orval J. Troy, Iqaluit, Northwest
  Territories
Barbara Tuck, Thornhill, Ontario
Charles P. Tuck, Oakville, Ontario
Dorothy Turcotte, Grimsby, Ontario
T. Daniel Tweel, Charlottetown, Prince
  Edward Island
Alberta Unger, Edmonton, Alberta
George C. Vandenberg, Sarnia, Ontario
John H. Van Steinburg, Kimberley, British
  Columbia
Ellen J. Vezina, London, Ontario
Mr. Justice Allan Wachowich, Edmonton,
  Alberta
Michael T. Wadsworth, Q.C., Toronto,
  Ontario
Peter I. Waldmann, Toronto, Ontario
Harvey G. Walker, North Battleford,
  Saskatchewan
R. Bryan Waller, Q.C., Calgary, Alberta
John T. Walsh, Stratford, Ontario
Donald J. Warner, Q.C., Lindsay, Ontario
Audrey E. Watson, Batawa, Ontario
Donald B. Webster, Toronto, Ontario
Judge Norris Weisman, Islington, Ontario
D. J. Welbourn, Claresholm, Alberta
Michael F. Welsh, Sechelt, British
  Columbia
Judge Arthur C. Whealy, Toronto, Ontario
Woodrow Wheatley, Parkdale, Prince
  Edward Island
Judge Walder White, Edmonton, Alberta
Roger Wilkinson, Oakville, Ontario
Deborah Wilson, Ottawa, Ontario
Douglas C. Woolley, Q.C., Toronto,
  Ontario
Judge Edward F. Wren, Toronto, Ontario
Jack Wylie, Kingston, Ontario
Roy Yerex, Winnipeg, Manitoba
David L. Youngson, Vancouver, British
  Columbia
A. John Zadoo, Toronto, Ontario
Daphne Zander, Pembroke, Ontario
Arnold H. Zweig, Toronto, Ontario